Diary of a Victorian Gardener

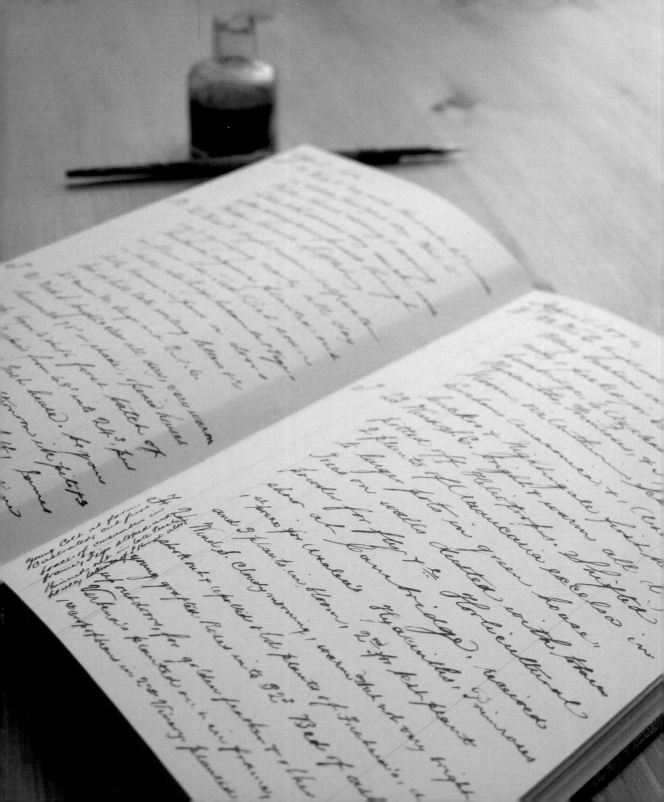

Diary of a Victorian Gardener

William Cresswell and Audley End

ENGLISH HERITAGE

Published by English Heritage,
NMRC, Kemble Drive, Swindon SN2 2GZ
www.english-heritage.org.uk

Copyright © English Heritage 2006

10 9 8 7 6 5 4 3 2 1

ISBN-10 1 85074 988 4
ISBN-13 978 1 85074 988 2

Product code 50999

A CIP catalogue for this book is available from the British Library

Edited and brought to press by Susan Kelleher
Designed by Pauline Hull
Printed by Bath Press

Contents

Preface

One very wet afternoon whilst driving and listening to Radio 4's *Food* programme, I heard the name William Cresswell mentioned. His diary, written in 1874 when he was a young man of 21 working in the garden of Audley End House, had recently been found. I felt a 'quickening' and that part of me that is him responded, reliving the memories of his enduring presence which he had left in his daughter Susan Alice (Susie) – my lovely granny.

I often visited granny spending days at a time with her during the school holidays. We had breakfast together in her soft feather bed – always wafer-thin bread and butter with her homemade marmalade and delicate tea in fine bone-china cups. On her bedside table, in a little leather pouch, was William's pocket watch. Every morning I saw her check it, carefully wind it, and gently replace it in the pouch. It was a little ritual which epitomised her emotions of tenderness, love and loss. In the quiet of those early mornings alone together she told me many things about her young life at Bowling Green Lodge (where William became Head Gardener later in his life) and her memories of William, whom she adored.

William was, as his father before him, a great educator; whilst granny did the darning and sewing for her mother in the evenings William sat with her, cat on lap, and taught her to recite huge passages from Shakespeare, Marcus Aurelius and Wordsworth (her favourite), and many psalms. These she remembered and loved all her life.

William also inspired a love of horticulture in granny as he did with many other people. One day, when in her eighties, she took me around her garden and introduced me to all the plants, giving me their common and full Latin names. I can just imagine William taking Susie by the hand and walking around the huge grounds of Bowling Green House and showing her the many and beautiful plants, shrubs and trees that he had nurtured and telling her their horticultural origins and names.

William wrote a very touching letter to Susie on her 21st birthday in 1897. He writes of his pride and satisfaction in her progress in life and their gift of a watch guard as a token of their 'affectionate regard for you, our high appreciation of your capabilities and conduct and our unceasing love for you'.

William loved walking – and granny did too. His diary entries often mention his visits to churches and flower shows etc some distances away. His parents lived in Grantchester and his girlfriend, Eliza Carlton, in Cambridge. Granny told me of her love of that city and her pleasure walking across the fields from Grantchester to the 'Backs'.

Lizzie – William's only sister – went back to Grantchester to visit family every year taking her granddaughter Margaret with her. Margaret remembers meeting William there and describes him as being a quiet, modest and gentle person.

William had a huge garden to manage at Bowling Green House. He once wrote, 'the abundance of work presses so hard on the smallness of time'. But when he finally had to retire he must have been bereft without his garden. William only lived a few years in retirement but his love of nature and passion for gardening lived on in his daughter Susie. Her daughters Beatrice and Betty (Evelyn) were talented pianists and Shakespearean actresses respectively, before the war turned them to more practical careers of family and nursing. My own children are pursuing careers in organic farming, music and English literature. As the well-known scientist and author, Steve Jones, wrote: 'We are all living fossils of our ancestors.'

Being reunited with William, his diary and recalling childhood memories of his daughter's love and reverence for him has been a marvellous personal experience. The kindness and diligence that Susan Kelleher of English Heritage has given to this book is truly amazing. It is wonderful to think that William's contribution to Audley End House in his youth, is still appreciated by many and has been preserved for us all by English Heritage.

Patricia Beatrice Rabôt
William Cresswell's great granddaughter

A portrait of William Cresswell by Quincy Rabôt

Introduction

David Baxter always looked forward to Mondays – that was the day when he took a little longer over lunch to enjoy the collectors' cornucopia offered by the bustling stalls of Covent Garden Market. One Monday in 1990 he stopped to pick up a little book with board covers assuming it was just a notebook, but was intrigued to discover that it was a diary recording the daily life of a Victorian gardener. Written in beautiful, copperplate handwriting, it only covered a couple of years but references leapt from the pages and struck a chord with David – Crystal Palace, Cambridge, Grantchester, Audley End. Not having time to study the diary at length, David decided the curious book was worth the few pounds asking price, so he paid up and pocketed the diary.

It was only when he had had time to read the book that he recognised its significance – here was a slice of Victorian social history centred round Audley End House in Essex, one of the most important houses in the country. A Jacobean 'prodigy' house built on the site of a 12th-century abbey, the magnificent mansion had been built to impress royalty and indeed later became a royal palace owned by King Charles II. Now under the guardianship of English Heritage and open to the public, Audley End was the place where much of the diary was written.

It was penned by a young gardener called William Cresswell who came to work in the large walled Kitchen Garden at the heart of the estate in 1874. A native of the Cambridgeshire village of Grantchester, he was an educated and sensitive man, keeping the diary to record his daily duties – but at the same time revealing much about his own character and the people he loved.

David Baxter decided that it would be fitting if the diary could return to the place where much of it was written – and so he kindly donated it to English Heritage. By coincidence, English Heritage was planning to restore the walled Kitchen Garden which had been radically changed and altered when the gardens were leased to a market garden business after the Second World War. The old glasshouses and other buildings that had been so fine in William Cresswell's day had either collapsed or were rotten and the whole Kitchen Garden was in a state of neglect. William Cresswell's diary was immediately crucial to this restoration, studied by landscape historians and horticulturalists – and acted upon.

The timely discovery of the diary is just one of a whole string of fortunate coincidences that have produced this book. And, just as William Cresswell's diary has played centre stage in the wonderful reconstruction of the walled Kitchen Garden at Audley End, so his complete, unaltered diary takes centre stage in this book. His words, punctuation and spelling remain as they were originally written, and a detailed commentary explains as much as possible about the gardening techniques, places and people he writes about. The life history of William Cresswell has been researched and is included, as well as a section on how Cresswell's diary proved so crucial for the Kitchen Garden restoration at Audley End.

As is revealed in William Cresswell's biography, he was a consummate gardener passionately devoted to his work. He would no doubt be delighted and honoured that it was his diary that has provided essential evidence for restoring the splendour of the gardens at Audley End, and that visitors today can enjoy and admire the same flowers, trees and buildings that he once did. And perhaps he would be surprised that the careful diary he kept as part of his work as a professional horticulturalist in the 19th century is still read, enjoyed and appreciated by people living in the 21st century.

William Cresswell

his life and work

WHEN WILLIAM CRESSWELL opened the first page of his little notebook, took the quill from his white porcupine-quill penholder and began to write, he was about to celebrate his 21st birthday. He was a young man taking the first steps in his career, and he cannot have imagined the interest his words would attract more than a century later. Cresswell was born on 25 February 1852 in the Cambridgeshire village of Grantchester, the second son of Susan and James Cresswell who lived next to the church in Clerk's Cottage (also known as Church Cottage). James Cresswell was a professional gardener and also the Assistant Parish Clerk, a man who was devoted to both aspects of his work and who seems to have imbued William with his own love of gardening and fervent Christian beliefs.

James and Susan had a family of six sons and one daughter – Henry, William, Frederick, Susan Elizabeth (known as Lizzie), George, John and James. It was a close-knit and loving family and all its members seem to have been very musical. James, the youngest son, played the organ in Grantchester church for many years, George became an organ builder and John a piano tuner. It is evident from his diary that William took great pleasure in music and singing, often recording the hymn tunes that had been played at Sunday services as well as sometimes commenting on the standards of the choir!

Although they were probably initially taught at home, William and his brothers and sister later attended the local school – a small, one-roomed thatched building just a short walk from their home. This had been built in 1830 and was later described as 'a very neat and pretty little room for the education of the children of the poorer classes'. In the 1850s a well-qualified teacher, Miss Charlotte Snelling, was in charge and the school

Opposite, top: Grantchester church with Church (or Clerk's) Cottage, the home of the Cresswell family for many years, to the right; below: As James, William Cresswell's father was the Clerk to the church, he was granted the cottage to live in; previous page: The Bothy, where William wrote his diary, is now presented as it would have looked in his day

12

GRANCHESTER SCHOOL

was attracting so many pupils that the little room soon became overcrowded. So the village ran a fund-raising campaign to build a larger school, which opened across the road with great ceremony in May 1867, with Miss Snelling as its headmistress.

William was a bright boy and his love of books and beautiful copperplate hand were the result of a good education and upbringing. He was ambitious and keen to learn and it is quite probable that this elementary education was supplemented by some music lessons given by Miss Lally Smith who took a few pupils at the Old Vicarage, down near the river. If so, he would have received an impression of quite remarkable intellectual vivacity. The three occupants of that house – Samuel Page Widnall, his wife and her sister, Lally Smith – were deeply interested in every new development in the world outside their quiet village. There was always something going on in that household, whether play-acting, adding romantic structures to the gardens, inventions of gadgetry, writing, photography or Lally's music. Perhaps William became caught up for a time in this wonderland.

When William left school he became an apprentice gardener, probably working for his father. This was very different from a jobbing gardener – William was making horticulture his career. Great advances in science and technology from the early 19th century meant that gardening had become established as a professional career and a whole system of apprenticeship and training grew up for those with ambitions. After serving an apprenticeship locally, the career gardener was expected to move on to a 'journeyman' position where he was paid by the day or 'journée'. He was expected to have gone through a course of

Opposite, top left: The one-roomed thatched village school at Grantchester; top right: William Cresswell and his brothers and sister are likely to have received their education at the village school to the right of this photograph; below left: Pupils of Grantchester School in the late 1890s; below right: Lally Smith who ran a small school at the Old Vicarage in the 19th century

Right: The old school still serves the village and is now used as part of the Village Hall

15

practical geometry and land surveying, have a scientific knowledge of botany and spend days and nights in studying books connected with his profession. Keeping a diary of his work was part of his training, useful as a reference for the gardener himself but also to show his employers what he was achieving (something professional gardeners still do today). Young gardeners with ambition needed to seek out the best gardens to broaden their experience, staying only a year or two to acquire new skills. William needed to gain a wide variety of experience to achieve his ultimate goal of becoming a head gardener.

At the age of 19 William was still living at home and is listed in the 1871 census as a gardener. Soon afterwards he left Grantchester and, by the time the diary begins in February 1873, William had achieved an important step-up in his career and been appointed a journeyman gardener for Mr and Mrs Yeo. The Yeos lived in a large, Georgian house called Elm Lodge which stood on the western side of Streatham High Road

Streatham Village painted by Augustus Charles Wyatt in 1879. It shows the rear of the ancient cottages known as Bedford Row with the spire of the parish church of St Leonard's rising above the tree-lined horizon. This is a view that would have been very familiar to William Cresswell but it was to vanish by the 1880s due to building development

(on the site now occupied by the junction of Penistone and Streatham High Roads). This was in Streatham, an up-and-coming area on the outskirts of London where many prestigious villas were being built by wealthy merchants, bankers and businessmen who wanted to live in the country but still be close to London. However, the area was still essentially rural and the Yeos had hayfields and farmland which William worked on, as well as maintaining both the flower and kitchen gardens. The gardens totalled some 3 acres – a large garden to the west of the house was laid out with lawns and shrubberies which were well stocked with mature trees. On the north wall were greenhouses and vineries and at the western end of the garden, screened by shrubs and bushes, were a number of outbuildings which probably included a potting shed. There was also a large glass conservatory attached to the house which enjoyed magnificent views of the surrounding countryside. To the south was a yard with stables and outbuildings with an arch leading through to the paddocks. Mr Yeo took a very personal interest in the running of the estate – William's diary records him supplying William with a hosepipe and making up seed orders with him as well as going to bulb sales, travelling together, as William carefully notes on 13 September 1873, in Mr Yeo's carriage. William seems to have had an excellent relationship with Mr Yeo and was given a great deal of responsibility.

One person is mentioned more than any other in the diary though her full name is never given. E.A.C. stands for Eliza Ann Carlton, a young girl from Cambridge who William was courting. In 1871 Eliza was working as a housemaid for the Revd William Martin at the Vicarage in Grantchester and they may have met around this time. William records her gift of a book and a letter for his 21st birthday and, although he never reveals it in so many words in the diary, it is obvious that he is deeply committed to the relationship. William records walking

An old map of Streatham showing Elm Lodge where William Cresswell was working when he began his diary

her home to Cambridge, trips to the seaside as well as more unusual outings such as the starlit night when he takes her to Grantchester Mill, where they were each weighed in turn on the scales used normally for sacks of grain! While he was away from Grantchester, the couple corresponded regularly and met up as often as possible, for example between 17 and 25 August 1873 when Eliza was obviously staying in London for a while. William writes in his diary about escorting her to such famous landmarks as the Houses of Parliament, Kew Gardens and Covent Garden. He also takes her to church because he is a strongly committed Christian, often going to church three times on a Sunday. As well as his religious beliefs, William also records signing the pledge and becoming a teetotaller. He is revealed as a man with great integrity and strength of character; a man who has not only faith in God but faith in himself.

William was not in a position to offer marriage to Eliza until he achieved the position of Head Gardener. The chances of any such promotion seemed bleak when on 29 September 1873 William was given notice to leave the Yeos (though no reason for this is clear from the diary). Gardeners often moved on quickly once they had learnt as much as they could from a position, and it was understood that they would need new challenges. Maybe the Yeos felt William had outgrown their relatively small estate, though perhaps the lecture on obedience he received on 18 September had something to do with it.

William assiduously wrote to various nurseries in the area and two weeks later began work at Carters of Forest Hill, a large professional nursery in south London. With typical generosity he shared his good fortune in obtaining work by giving a shilling to a man he met who was searching for employment. Carters were to provide William with a new range of skills and he quickly became involved in fulfilling a frantic round of orders for the thriving business. However he did not remain at Carters

Eliza Ann Carlton

for very long as, by March 1874, William had achieved a most prestigious appointment – as a gardener at Audley End House in Essex, the home of Lord and Lady Braybrooke. This magnificent mansion set in vast acres of parkland with formal and kitchen gardens, was a dream location for the young gardener only a few miles from his childhood home in Grantchester – where his family and sweetheart still lived. He may have been recommended for this position by William Chater, who owned a large nursery in Saffron Walden that supplied the Audley End estate.

William Cresswell probably took over from William Newman who was earning 2s 8d a day working as 2nd man in the Audley End Kitchen Garden in 1873, under Mr Bryan, the Head Gardener. Newman was appointed in late 1872 but a letter written by Lady Braybrooke to her land agent on 12 March 1874 reveals that she had reservations about his abilities, feeling he was 'not equal to the situation, having had no

Audley End House, a magnificent mansion set in extensive gardens and parkland

experience except in our garden'. Unbeknown to her, William Cresswell had already taken his place.

This was a definite advancement in William's career and only one step away from his ultimate goal of Head Gardener, and he had to work very hard. The hours were long and wages low. William earned 16 shillings a week when he started and an account of 1873 reveals that the men worked 313 days of the year with no holidays and only Sundays off. The under-gardeners also took turns working on a Sunday to see to watering, heating and ventilation. The unmarried gardeners lived in the Bothy, rooms at the back of the Vinery range where they were on hand to keep a constant check on the vineries and glasshouses. William probably shared this accommodation with James Bedgegood, the 3rd man, and they would have cooked for themselves, although clean linen was supplied by the 'garden women'.

In his position as 2nd man, William would have been in charge of several gardeners though he reveals little of this side of his job in the diary. This implies that relationships with other members of the staff were good; indeed, William records suppers and cricket matches with his colleagues with evident enjoyment. There was, however, some tension in his dealings with Mr Bryan, the Head Gardener. Matters came to a head on 20 July when visitors arrived wanting to look round the garden. Mr Bryan could not be found and William felt perfectly justified in showing them round himself. Mr Bryan was 'angry' when he found out and William was dismayed to be told off for his actions. He confided to his diary that this was almost the final straw and he was seriously thinking of handing in his notice. He must have been very torn – his emplyment at Audley End was invaluable experience for him and he appeared to enjoy the wide range of work he was doing. Although much involved in the care of the fruit and vegetable parts of the

gardens, it was as a flower specialist that he particularly excelled. It is evident that he had great skills in propagating, planting and arranging the floral displays, and he also uses the correct names for plants when writing about them. On 11 September 1874 he records putting in cuttings of *Stellaria graminea aurea* showing that he was knowledgeable about the most up-to-date species. His diary records with justifiable pride how the flowers, fruit and vegetables he has grown in the gardens win prizes at the local horticultural shows. His love of flowers is further revealed from the brief note on 30 March telling how he got up early to gather dew-fresh violets, and his record of taking the flowers up to the house to decorate Lady Braybrooke's sitting room on 16 July. The pleasures of his job obviously outweighed the difficulties in his dealings with Mr Bryan at that time because William decided to stay.

In the end it was Mr Bryan who took the decision, as William records on 31 August that he has been given a month's notice. Contracts were being re-negotiated in 1874 on the retirement of Mr Young, Head Gardener of the pleasure grounds, and Mr Bryan was to take over as Head Gardener of the whole Audley End estate. There seems to have been no ill-feeling between William and Mr Bryan and indeed Mr Bryan gave William a 'letter of recommendation' to accompany his application for a job at Veitch's Nursery in London – probably the best nursery in the country at that time. Unfortunately he didn't receive an offer of employment from them and, on 30 September, William records packing his box and leaving Audley End and the service of Lord Braybrooke.

He returned home to Grantchester and continued searching for full-time employment while doing some part-time work for friends and family. On 29 October he called at the Cambridge Botanic Gardens to see the Curator, Mr Mudd, and this interview led to the offer of a job. At this point William's

Opposite: Lady Braybrooke's sitting room in Audley End House is presented in the way it would have looked in the 1870s

diary ends, his last entry being a note of the grisly murder case that had been gripping the nation. However, using census returns, family memories, parish records and the resources of local history study centres, it has been possible to piece together the rest of William's life story.

William began work at the Botanic Gardens on 9 November and received his first weekly payment of 16 shillings on 5 December 1874. He obviously did well because five months later his pay had increased to 17 shillings and then to £1 1s on 25 September 1875. He was also appointed Assistant Curator when Mr Mudd's son, who had held that position, left. This was rapid promotion over other gardeners who had been working at the Botanic Gardens for longer. Nevertheless, William left soon after, receiving his last pay on 22 January 1876. He may well have secured a position as Head Gardener – although he would have been very young to have achieved this status, William did have extensive and varied experience.

William must have been a Head Gardener later in 1876 because he and Eliza were finally married on 26 October 1876 in Grantchester. Eliza's address was given as Grantchester and she was probably still working at the Vicarage, but William's

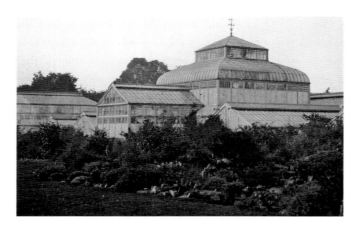

Botanic Gardens, Cambridge, in the Victorian period

address was given as All Saints in Upper Norwood, south London. He may well have already obtained his position at nearby Windermere House, a large house in Croydon. This had extensive grounds which have now been incorporated into the present-day Westow Park, and a Gardener's House where William was living by the 1881 census. These must have been happy times for William – he had at last married Eliza, he had his own home and an excellent job. On 4 August 1877 a further joy: William and Eliza's daughter Susan was born, named after William's beloved mother. Two other children were born while they were living in the Upper Norwood area – Ethel on 1 January 1880 and William Carlton on 24 November 1881.

By the time Lucy Emma was born on 31 March 1885, William was working at Bowling Green House in Putney. This prestigious house got its name as it had been adapted from a former bowling green house, a place where large social gatherings and entertainments were held in the early 18th century. Situated on Putney Heath, north of Wimbledon Common, the house became famous as the residence of William Pitt the Younger who had become the country's youngest ever Prime Minister in 1783, at the age of only 24. His house at Putney had over 5 acres of landscaped gardens which were particularly noted for the many varieties of rhododendrons growing there. The grounds also had areas of managed woodland with paths meandering through – one of which was known as 'Pitt's Walk'.

In 1885 Bowling Green House became the home of Henry Lewis Doulton who had worked for his father Sir Henry Doulton at the famous pottery and ceramics company since 1873. He became a partner in 1881 and head of the firm in 1897 on the death of his father. Bowling Green House was convenient for Lambeth where the company had been founded

A treasured locket still in the possession of the family with portraits of William and Eliza at around the time of their marriage

in 1815 and where their headquarters still are. William and Eliza lived in the Lodge on the estate and soon added two more children to their bustling household – Henry James (born 4 September 1887) and Constance (born 25 August 1893). William's employer continued to live at Bowling Green House until his death in 1930 when the estate was put up for sale. A strenuous campaign to have the house bought by the National Trust or used as a museum failed. Bowling Green House was demolished and William's beloved gardens built over. Today only the coachman's house and stables still remain and part of the wall that probably once surrounded the kitchen gardens.

William retired to live nearby with Eliza and his youngest unmarried daughter, Constance, at 76 Pulborough Road, Southfields. He was devastated by the loss of the beautiful house and the gardens which he had tended for so many years, and he was also increasingly worried about Eliza who was showing symptoms of Alzheimer's Disease. William's health began to fail under the strain and he suffered from acute angina. As Constance had a full-time job working in central London and was away from home every day, much of the responsibility for caring for Eliza fell on William. He coped with his usual fortitude and resilience buoyed by his fervent faith, but it must have been very difficult for him. William's angina attacks became stronger and more severe and in October 1930 he went into hospital for a short while. Although back at home by January 1931 he was still very weak and became increasingly frail. On the evening of Sunday 4 January he went out for his usual Sunday walk – a habit he had enjoyed for most of his life and often recorded in his diary written over 50 years earlier. Walking along a path by the railway line at Southfields, he seems to have suffered a heart attack and was found collapsed by the track with his right arm across the live rail. Two men dragged him clear and gave him artificial respiration until the

Opposite, top: An etching of 'Pitt's Walk' at Bowling Green House; **below:** *Bowling Green House shortly before its demolition*

27

ambulance arrived. William was taken to St James's Hospital, Balham, where his burns and broken arm were treated. He made good progress in hospital as the burns were only superficial but he suddenly collapsed and died on 22 January. The coroner's inquest that followed recorded that he had died from natural causes connected with his heart condition and that the injuries he had received had not contributed to his death. William's wife battled with her illness for several more years, dying at home on 1 May 1939 at the age of 90.

When William laid his pen down for the last time in 1875 and closed his little book, he must have wondered what life would have in store for him. As it happened he achieved everything he wanted – a happy marriage; children and grandchildren; and a respected position at the top of his profession. It was only when the gardening had to stop that things began to go wrong for William and he lost the confidence and optimism which had so characterised his early life, and which shine through his diary. Hopefully, he kept that little diary close to him in his latter years as a constant reminder of his achievements.

Opposite: William Cresswell in his sixties, still wearing his watch and chain. He was known as a lover of nature and one of nature's natural gentlemen; **below:** *The first page of the diary he began a few days before his 21st birthday*

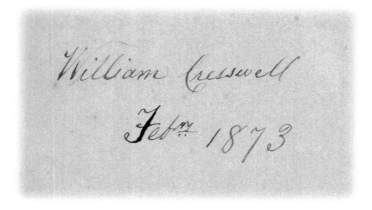

June 1873

F 17 Fine day very warm. Shifted Amaranthus
      &c &c into 24 sized. putting out
      Celery. cut away shoots in borders to
      make room for a row of bedding plants
      Had Gardeners from Miss Lloyds
      Mr Yeo Son &c

W 18 heavy rain in morning. cloudy greater
      part of day very warm. Shelves on for
      Conservatory G Amaranthus. Mignonette
      Zonal Geraniums. Ageratum &c &c Lobelia
      Stoped and thinned vines in late houses

T 19 Wind W fine morning. rain in afternoon
      Pulling out more bedding plants in
      borders & filling up vacancies in beds
      where others had died.

F 20 Wind S.W dull but bright & warm. Mowed lawn
      all over. finished bedding out. Potted off
      first lot of Cineraria's. put in cold frame

S 21 Wind S.W rather dull. very close & warm
      Potted off Centaurea & c Cineraria maritima
      Candidissima. Tussen van Vlissen. Gathered first
      lot of Peas of the first crop sown the beginning
      of Feby Variety Sangsters No 1. forced early frame

June 1873

S 22 W. N.W fine day went to the church
      Mr & E Sutton sang at each service
      very touching & effective sermon preached
      in M by Revd Stenton Eardley from John 1 v 28 &c

M 23 Wind N.W fine not very bright. Cleared out
      pit where Potatos have been growing, to be
      ready for cucumbers and Melons

T 24 Wind N.W dull few showers of rain
      Cleaning up conservatory, introducing
      Fuschia's. Hydrangeas. Ferns & Pelargoniums
      Large frame filled with hot dung
      for Cucumbers & Melons. Mr Y— Son arrived

W 25 Wind N.W cloudy. fine evening.
      Pulled weeds out from seed beds of winter
      greens. celery. Endive & 2nd sowing between currants

T 26 Wind N.W fine Morning. a few drops of
      rain in Middle of day. dull later part
      howing between crops. Got in peat
      for potting hard wooded plants

F 27 Wind N.W very warm & bright. Potted
      Heaths & Epacrises keeping them in doors
      mowed lawn Hoed flower beds & borders. watered
      seed beds of Vegetables & celery in trenches

Diary

William Cresswell wrote his diary in a distinctive copperplate
which is sometimes quite difficult to decipher.
This transcription has followed the original keeping William's
spelling and punctuation. There are many abbreviations in the
diary for people's names and places,
eg C–ge for Cambridge; M. & E. for morning and evening;
P. & N. for pruning and nailing; I.C. for Immanuel Church etc.
As we wanted to publish the diary in as entire a form as possible,
all these abbreviations have been left as the original.

FEBRUARY 1873

Monday 18 –
Friday 21

Arrainging plants in greenhouses, Conservatory &c. Laxtons Supreme Peas sown 21st with Spinach. Weather dull no sun, frosty.

Saturday 22

Put in cuttings of Lobelia's. Fuschias potted off cuttings of Fuschias, stood them in Early vinery. W. dull morning, sun shining in middle of day afternoon dull followed by rain at night.

Sunday 23

Showery morning, bright afternoon, rain at night. Went to church Morning & Evening. Sermons preached for Missions by Revd. Adams gave 6d. Went to Crystal Pallace in the afternoon, had tea with Mr. and Mrs. Farrow.

Monday 24

Cold morning, ground covered with snow and continued to fall all day. Potted 1 doz zonal geraniums into 48 size pots to bloom early for Conservatory, began cleaning bedding plants.

Tuesday 25

Wet day, thawing fast. Same time cleaning bedding plants indoors. My 21st birthday. Received a letter & a book each from E.A.C. & H.C. Received notices from Rees. Sent letter to Mr. Smith also to Mr. Chater, with photograph of self. Posted latter next morning.

Wednesday 26

Mild. Showery day. Finished cleaning bedding geraniums. Potted 2 Peach trees which had been lying out of doors put in greenhouse. Potted yellow calceolarias in 48 size pots for early flowering for Conservatory. Got in peat for ferns.

Thursday 27

Mild, little sun, few showers of rain. Pruning Gooseberries & Currants. Made up order for seeds with Mr. Yeo. Recieved by post seed catalogue from J.J. Chater.

Friday 28

Dull morning, slight fall of snow during the night with little frost. Sun shining the rest part of day. Pruning & nailing wall trees.

MARCH 1873

Saturday 1 Wind S. rained all day. Repotting Ferns shifted Pilea muscosa into 48 size pots. Sowed several sorts of flower seeds viz. Solanum, Lobelia, Ageratum Centaurea raqusina, P. Golden Feather.

Sunday 2 Wind N.W. dull morning bright afternoon. Went to Streatham Hill Church morning & night. Walked to Croydon & back in afternoon.

Monday 3 Wind S.W. dull, no sun, few showers. Fresh plants put in Conservatory, hyacinths put in heat, others which have been plunged got indoors. Ground dug for Onion bed. Pruning & nailing on walls.

Tuesday 4 Very mild. Sun in middle of day. Air given to all houses and frames. Pig killed. Bed partly prepared for cucumbers in c. house. Self pruning and nailing wall trees.

Wednesday 5 Wind S.W. Rained all day little or much. Repaired Potting bench. Sowed seeds of Mignonette dwarf compact & hybrid tree Cucumber bed finished. Pruning & nailing a few hours.

Thursday 6 Wind S.W. dull morning, cold wind. Sun middle of day, dull afternoon. Tyed down laterals of early vines. Pruning & nailing on walls.

Friday 7 Rained fast till 11 o'clock, rest part of day fine, rather cloudy, little sun, rather strong wind blowing from S.W., very cold. Put in pot of cuttings of lobelia, repotted Ferns.1 Azalea put in heat. P & N wall trees.

Saturday 8 Wind S.W. cold & stormy. Received from M^r. Yeo 6 Bell glasses, 1lb tobacco paper, 1/2 peck Early Rose, 1 peck Rivers Royal Ash leaf Potatoes.

Sunday 9 Wind W. bright morning, followed by rain in showers. Went to church Morning & evening. M. S. Common, E. S. Hill.

Monday 10 Wind S.W. cold & stormy, few showers of hail. Pruned plums on North wall, cut largest tubers of Early Rose potatoes in early vinery, took out Hyacinths and put in Conservatory, brought in others from cool house. Smoked Pelargoniums & plants in early vinery.

Diary 1873

February 18. 19. 20. 21 M. T. W. T. F.

Arranging plants in greenhouses
Conservatory & Laxtons Supreme Peas sown
21st with Spinach. Weather dull no sun frosty

S 22 Put in cuttings of Lobelia's. Fuschias
potted off cuttings of Fuschias. stood them
in Early vinery. W. dull morning. sun shining in
middle of day afternoon dull followed by rain at night

S 23 Showery morning. bright afternoon. rain at Night
went to church Morning & Evening. Sermons
preached for Missions by Revd Adams gave 6°
went to crystal Pallace in the afternoon
had Tea with Mr and Mrs Farrow

M 24 Cold Morning ground covered with Snow
and continued to fall all day. Potted 1 doz
Zonal geraniums into 48 size pots to bloom

W	26	Mild. Showery day finished cleaning bedding geraniums Potted 2 Peach trees which had been lying out of doors put in greenhouse Potted yellow calceolarias in 48 size pots for early flowering for Conservatory. Got in Peat for ferns
T	27	Mild. little sun. few showers of rain Pruning Gooseberries & Currants. Made up order for Seeds with Mr Yeo. Recieved by post seed catalogue from J. J. Chater
F	28	Dull morning slight fall of snow during the night with little frost. Sun shining the rest part of day. Pruning & nailing wall trees
March S	1st	Wind S. rained all day Repotting Ferns shifted Pilea muscosa into 48 size pots. Sowed several sorts of Flower seeds viz. Solanum Lobelia. Ageratum. Centaurea ragusina P. Golden Feather.
S	2	Wind N. W. dull morning bright afternoon

Tuesday 11	Weather same as yesterday. Glass put in Conservatory, frames repaired with glass. Potting ferns. Pruning & nailing.
Wednesday 12	Wind N. dull cloudy morning, middle of day bright with sun. Filled pots with peat soil for fern spores and cuttings of Lycopodium. Ground dug between Gooseberry & Currant bushes. Pruning & nailing on walls. Smoked Pelargoniums.
Thursday 13	Wind N. ground covered with snow, thawed very fast, little sun in middle of day. Put in cuttings of Selaginella caesia and stoloniferum also stephanotis and Eschynanthus. Sowed fern spores under bell glass. Potting shed cleaned out, pots put in order. Coke came in.
Friday 14	Wind N. Sharp frost. Got up plants for table for dinner party. Flue from large boiler cleaned out and repaired. Pruning & nailing on walls. Received from M^r. Yeo 2 new watering pots.
Saturday 15	Very cold day. Wind E. changing occasionally to N.E. Sowed mustard & cress under stage in early vinery. Potted tubers of Achimenes, cleaned Pelargoniums, Cinerarias, Calceolarias &c. Cut down Oleander. Pinched tops off bedding Calceolarias.
Sunday 16	Wind E. very cold and wet. Went to Immanuel Church Morning & Evening. Stayed indoors all the afternoon, wrote names of tunes in A & M Hymn Book.
Monday 17	Wind N. dull morning, very warm in middle of day with sun continuing till night. Put in 3 pots of cuttings of Heliotropes, also cuttings of Dahlias. Asparagus beds forked over. Pruning & nailing on walls. Went to singing class, proposed & seconded as a member, agreed, payed yearly subscription 2/-.
Tuesday 18	Wind N. dull damp day. P & N on walls. Beck's dwarf green gem beans planted.
Wednesday 19	Wind N.E. high, very cold, but drying, cloudy & sunless. Pruning and nailing wall trees.
Thursday 20	A very drying wind from N.E. with a few light showers, hardly any sun. Pruning & nailing wall trees now coming into bloom. Holes in lawn rectified. Large sets of River's Royal Ashleaf potatoes cut, lying in early vinery to forward them.

Friday 21   Wind N.E. very cold and stormy (rain, hail & snow) melted as fast as it fell. Rearrainged plants in conservatory &c. Lawn swept and rolled.

Saturday 22   Wind E. little frost in morning, bright, clear and fine all day. Potting ferns and arranging plants in Early Vinery. Walked to Brixton & back in the evening.

Sunday 23   Wet cloudy morning. Afternoon clear and bright. Went to Immanuel Church morning and evening. Stayed in all afternoon, had tea alone. Sat in church with singers 1st time.

Monday 24   Dull & foggy first in the morning changing to a bright sunny & warm day. Beet seed sown. Planted out Early Rose Potatoes which had been started in heat. Sowed seeds in pots in early vinery of Acacia lophantha & coecinea. Gloxinia, Cyclamen, Centaurea, sensitive plant Celosia japonica, Calceolaria.

Tuesday 25   Wind N. lovely day. Thinned & stoped early vines & tyed them down. Pruning & nailing plums on north wall. Onion sowed. Hardy mammouth 'Giant Tripoli' and White Spanish.

Wednesday 26   Wind N.E. foggy morning bright & clear, very warm the rest part of the day. Sowed celery seed in box indoors also seeds of greenhouse plants & bedding var Perilla Amaranthus salicifolius & globe also Tomatoe seeds sown out of doors. Beet, Radio, Radish, Lettuce.

Thursday 27   Wind N.E. dull morning till 11 o'clock afterwards clear, sunny & warm. Potted off Fuschias also shifted young specimens into larger pots. Potted 2 Heliotropes for standards & put in cuttings of same.Early Potatoes planted out of doors, P & N Plums.

Friday 28   Wind N.E. little frost in morning, very foggy. Mild in middle of day with sun, slight fog all day. Put in cuttings of Lobelias & Dahlias. Pruned Roses. Seed sown of B.sprouts, cabbage & cauliflower. Cauliflowers (wintered in frame) planted out.

Saturday 29   Wind N.E. bright & warm. Put in cuttings of Lemon scented verbena.

Sunday 30	Wind N.E. beautiful bright & clear morning, rather dull in afternoon, raining fast in the evening. Went to Immanuel church Morning & Evening. Went to Norwood Cemetery in afternoon.
Monday 31	Wind W. dull & showery. Finished Pruning & nailing wall trees, began box edging.

APRIL 1873

Tuesday 1	Wind W. bright clear day very warm. Putting in box edging. Planted in border sweet Williams & wallflowers.
Wednesday 2	Wind W. slight frost in morning, very warm day. Sowed seed of Ageratum Tom Thumb. Pruned std fruit trees. Lawn mowed with scythe. Putting in box edging.
Thursday 3	Wind W. dull morning little rain. Cleaned plants in Conservatory. Brought out large cactus & put in late vinery. Got up plants & flowers for the table for dinner party.
Friday 4	Wind W. dull day rather showery. Cleaning plants in greenhouse. Cut back Erica hymalis, Epacris Libonia floribunda Corranilla &c. Smoked the house at night.
Saturday 5	Wind W. dull and showery. Put out shrubby Calceolarias from store boxes into cold frames. Planted cucumber plants in bed in C. house.
Sunday 6	Cold and stormy. Went to Immanuel Church M & E. Stayed in all afternoon reading.
Monday 7	Wind W. dull cold & stormy. Stopped & tyed down vines. Put out calceolarias in small pit where wintered after filling in some soil. Planted some out in borders. Cut 1st flowers from forced Roses.
Tuesday 8	Wind N.E. cold few showers. Finished planting in borders, shrubby calceolarias. Seeds sown of Antirrhinum. Kale sprouting brocoli, coleworts. Lettuce put out on vine border. Cabbage pricked out. Cleaning between Strawberries & Endive.

Wednesday 9	Wind N.E. no showers very drying. Plunged Lycopodium denticulatum (60 size) into 32s. Shifted Isolepis gracilis into 48s. Cleaned up conservatory introducing more Azaleas, Hyacinths, Auriculas & Cinerarias. Early horn carrot sowed on vine border. Began cutting lawn with machine for the 1st time.
Thursday 10	Wind N.E. fine day. Finished cutting lawn. Put rooted cuttings of Lobelias and Dahlias into cool vinery to harden off.
Friday 11	Good Friday. Wind N.E. very cold no sun, little rain in the evening. Went with Brother H. to Immanuel Church in morning, to C. Palace to a sacred concert in afternoon, heard Hallelujah Chorus on Large Organ.
Saturday 12	Wind & weather same as yesterday only warmer. Sowed seeds of Asters & Stock in heat.
Sunday 13	Dull morning, sun in afternoon. Went to I.C. in morning. Walked to L. bridge in afternoon, went to Spurgeon's Tabernacle in evening. Text 16 Numbers 48 verse.
Monday 14	Wind E. lovely day. Went to work first in the morning to water, open the houses &c, spent the rest of day in London, paid a visit to British Museum, Covent Garden market and other places (Bank holliday).
Tuesday 15	Wind E. very warm day. Henry went home (came on the 10th) – saw him from Streatham by 9.17 am train to L. Hill. Planted out Delphinium formosum in border which had been struck under handlight. More Potatoes planted.
Wednesday 16	Wind N.E. very warm, few peals of thunder in afternoon. Sowed first crop of Turnips & put in French beans Newington wonder 1st crop. Mr. Lloyd from Cambridge called.
Thursday 17	Wind N.E. rather warm, cloudy at times, few showers of rain latter part of day. Cleaning ferns in vinery & putting in box edging. Mr. & Mrs. Yeo returned from Brighton went out in evening to dinner party. Made up boquet for table & Camellias for hair which they took with them.

Friday 18	Wind N. very changable, heavy shower of rain in middle of day. Putting in box edging. Potted off Tomatoe the Trophy 4 doz into large 60 pots. Began tying down & thining laterals of vines in late houses.
Saturday 19	Wind N. bright & clear wind rather cold. Cleaned up conservatory, brought out exhausted Hyacinths & Primulas & took in Auriculas, Tulips, Cinerarias &c. Tyed down & stopped vines in early house, some of the fruit just coming into bloom. M^r. Yeo went out.
Sunday 20	Wind N. rather strong, clear with sun. Went to I. church M.E., very effective sermon preach in E. by Rev^d. Bradstock (brother to the curate) from the 15 of John 9, 10 verses.
Monday 21	Wind N.E. fine day. Mowed lawn with machine, dutch howed borders. Sowed seed of Single & Double Zinnia, & little cinerarias in heat.
Tuesday 22	Wind E. dull day. Potted off in 48s Hydrangea's (with bloom set in them) into 54s Telegraph cucumber. Divided and replanted old plants of P. G. Feather in borders cleaning border simultaneously.
Wednesday 23	Wind N.E. few showers of hail. Replanted Panseys in beds on lawn. Cut edges of grass.
Thursday 24	Wind N.E. sharp frost in morning, showers of rain, hail & snow during the day. Howing between raspberries, gooseberries &c. Potted off Celosia japonica into large 60 pots. Sticks put to earliest Peas.
Friday 25	The same
Saturday 26	Wind N.E. frost in morning. Went over vines in all the houses & thinned, stopped & tyed down the laterals. Potatoes planted.
Sunday 27	Wind W. dull rather showery. Went to Immanuel Church M & E. Rev^d. Griffiths preached both times. Tunes in the E. were Darwell, Miles Lane & Tallis.
Monday 28	Wind W. mild. Shifted Fuschias into larger pots. Potted off Perillas & Mignonette.

Tuesday 29	Wind N.E. mild showery morning, fine afternoon. Potted off Amaranthus salicifolius into small 60 pots. Cleaned up conservatory putting in Azaleas, Roses &c. Pruned Camellias, Epacris &c.
Wednesday 30	Wind W. mild not much sun. Sowed hardy annuals in border round lawn also border under wall at end of late vinerys. Turned bulbs (done flowering) out of pots & layed down in the ground to make room for other things.

MAY 1873

Thursday 1	Wind W. very warm. Rhubarb uncovered viz. manure taken away which had been put round to force it. Putting in box edging. Mr. & Mrs. Yeo returned.
Friday 2	Wind W. bright day very warm. Putting in box edging. Began mowing lawn. Put in two rows of Carters Surprise Peas at four feet apart height 3 feet with row of lettuce between them, Tom Thumb, some to transplant, others to remain where sown.
Saturday 3	Wind W. few showers of rain. Finished mowing lawn. Rolled gravel walks. Fetched home coat from London £2 10s 0d.
Sunday 4	Wind W. mild few showers in afternoon. Went to I. Church M. & E. took a walk to Tooting Common in afternoon.
Monday 5	Wind N.E. cold & showery. Potted off Solanum hybridum into large 60 pots, put on shelf in cucumber house. Pricked out or planted young spring sown (under glass) lettuce in vine border and between strawberries. Began disbudding Peaches & Apricots. Early cabbages planted out.
Tuesday 6	Wind W. fine day. Finished disbudding trees on walls. Potted off young seedlings of Ageratum Tom Thumb in small 60 pots. Pricked out ten week stocks & asters into cold frame. Giant White Runners planted in rows 6 feet apart.
Wednesday 7	Wind W. changeable. Sowed more French beans. Thinned grapes in early vinery just swelling off.

Thursday 8	Wind W. very showery. Put out young plants of P. Golden Feather from the seed pan for summer bedding.
Friday 9	Wind West fine day. Suffering with Bile on stomach, went to work after breakfast watered plants indoors and returned again not being able to keep on.
Saturday 10	Weather same as yesterday. Self not much better, went in afternoon & watered plants &c. Received full pay from Mr. Yeo. Mr. Farrow left for Cambridge.
Sunday 11 & Monday 12	Self unwell, not able to work, fine weather. Went to S.H. church on Sunday evening.
Tuesday 13	Wind N. very warm. Started to work again. Sowed seeds of Cabbage, B. sprouts, Savoy, Celery, Cauliflower, Brocoli, Kail for Autumn and winter use, also Endive for summer.
Wednesday 14	Wind N.E. dull day. Sowed first lot of Primula and 2nd crop of Turnips. Cleaned edge of vine border and path round them.
Thursday 15	Wind N.E. clear day. Stopped & thinned vines in late houses. Watered all the walks with boiling hot salt and water to kill the weeds.
Friday 16	Wind N.E. fine day. Staked Pelargoniums & Calceolarias for conservatory, cleaning latter. Smoked Pelargoniums & plants in cucumber house at night.
Saturday 17	Wind N.E. rather high few showers in afternoon. Sprinkled salt on surface of Asparagus beds & watered with liquid manure. Made up boquet for hand in collar for opera.
Sunday 18	Wind N.E. very dull & cold. Went to I. church M. & E. Lemon chant to psalms in E.
Monday 19	Wind N.E. dull & cold little sun in middle of day. Thinned early grapes 2nd time. Beet thinned and transplanted. Mushroom house cleared out and put in heap for the marrows.

Tuesday 20   Wind W. frost in morning fine day. Sowed mustard & cress & radish. Began mowing lawn with machine.

Wednesday 21   Wind W. dull showery day. Earthed up earliest Potatoes. Early horn carrot thinned. Shifted plants of Deutzia gracilis, Richardia Ethiopica and Auriculas. Potted off sensitive plants into large 60 pots.

Thursday 22   Wind W. dull morning bright rest of day. Finished cutting lawn. Began bedding out on star bed with Geraniums & Calceolarias. Potted off Globe Amaranthus also Acacia coceinea, some singly into large 60s (to be shifted into 48s when rooted) others in 16s. 16 in a pot to bloom for Conservatory. Seed sown of Mangel Wurzel.

Friday 23   Wind W. nice shower in morning. Sun shining rest part of day, strong wind. Potted off Vegetable Marrows in 54 pots.

Saturday 24   Wind W. fine warm day. Cut edges of grass round lawn & beds thereon & swept all walks. Shifted Amaranthus salicifolius into 48s and the largest of Celosia japonica into 32s. Dusted early grapes (just swelling off) with sulphur to kill mildew, also painted the pipes with a mixture of lime and sulphur, most of the latter.

Sunday 25   Wind W. lovely day. Sermons preached in Immanuel church M. & E. for Church Missions. Black clergyman preached in M. Went to Tooting in afternoon, saw W. Rollisson & Sons Nursery. Came home by Mitcham.

Monday 26   Wind W. fine day. Mowed lawn with machine. Carters Leviathan Peas sown. Made up boquet in collar.

Tuesday 27   Wind West. Showery day very warm, few peals of thunder in middle of day. Bedded out Lobelias, Geraniums, Ageratum. Received new india rubber pipes for watering.

Wednesday 28   Wind W. dull day. Gave vine border (inside early house) a good soaking with tepid water put out in beds lobelias, perilla, geraniums, calceolarias &c.

Thursday 29   Wind N.E. fine day. Tyed up earliest lettuces, gave bedding plants in beds a good watering with hose.

Friday 30 Wind N. dull day fine evening. Put out P. Golden Feather round margin of beds. Filled Vases on lawn, put out more bedding plants. Lettuce planted between strawberries.

Saturday 31 Wind W. fine day. Cut large piece of grass and clipped all edges. Changed lodgings.

JUNE 1873

Sunday 1 Wind W. Very showery. Went to I. church M. & E. (Whit Sunday). Chorus sung in evening from H. Messiah (And the Glory of the Lord).

Monday 2 Fine Day. Bank holliday. Large croquet party at Mr. Yeo's. Cleaned up Conservatory.

Tuesday 3 Wind W. Heavy rain in morning, rest part of day fine. Began getting out plants from houses. Pruned Genistas, stopped laterals on late vines and thinned out the leaves where too much crowded.

Wednesday 4 Wind N.W. very warm. Thunder storm in afternoon with heavy rain. Took up Myosotis and other things to make room for bedding plants. Put out Geraniums & Calceolarias. Late potatoes earthed up.

Thursday 5 Wind W. very dull & dark morning clearer with sun in afternoon. Stopped laterals of late vines and thinned out the leaves where too thick. Savoys planted out, B. sprouts pricked out. Potted up Asters & stocks for Conservatory into 32 pots 4 in a pot. Planted out others in beds and borders.

Friday 6 Wind N.W. very dull all day no sun. Finished planting out Stocks & Asters in borders. Finished planting all beds on lawns. Potted yellow Calceolarias into 32s for Conservatory. Stopped laterals of early vines, getting out ferns & clearing other plants in same.

Saturday 7 Wind N.W. Mowed Lawn all over with Machine.

Sunday 8 Wind N.W. dull morning fine afternoon & evening. Went to I. church in morning after dinner to London (Hyde Park), walked through Park, also R. Gardens.

Monday 9	Wind W. Finished cleaning Early Vinery, washed sulphur off with syringe. Took up (from borders) Iris and reduced others, throwing them away.
Tuesday 10	Wind W. dull day. Sowed seeds of Calceolaria, Cineraria & Primula. Took up Saxifraga cassifolia from border and throwed away, put out Geraniums & Perilla. Planted out Dahlias & Tomatoes, Scarlet Runners, Peas &c Staked. Fetched plants from W.G. large Myrtle, Herbaceous plants &c.
Wednesday 11	Wind W. warm day. Shifted Celosia japonica into 32s. Sowed seed of Viola (Mauve queen & Lutea). Finished putting out bedding plants round borders.
Thursday 12	Wind W. warm day. Removed Strawberries from top of vinery to bottom being in the way of the vines and took out all that had not fruit on. Planted out Vegetable Marrows & more Tomatoes. Cut down weeds in borders between Gooseberry & Currant bushes. Strawberries mulched with dry litter to preserve the fruit which is now swelling off.
Friday 13	Wind E. close & warm bright in morning, in afternoon rain with thunder & lightning. Shifted Solanum hybridum from large 60s some into 32s & some into 48s, planted others out in border howing between crops. Took Calceolarias & Geraniums to Mr. Yeo Tenants. Mowed lawn. Trained & stoped cucumbers.
Saturday 14	Fine day. Finished mowing lawn & cutting edges, swept walks &c.
Sunday 15	Rather dull. At I church M. & Evening.
Monday 16	Very warm. Putting out first crop of Celery sorts Sandringham, Hooleys Conqueror, gave it a good soaking of water also watered beds on lawn which were planted last.
Tuesday 17	Fine day, very warm. Shifted Amaranthus salicifolius into 24s. Finished putting out Celery. Cut away shrubs in borders to make room for a row of bedding plants. Had Anthesas from Miss Lloyds. Mr. Yeo's son died.
Wednesday 18	Heavy rain in morning, cloudy greater part of day, very warm. Shifted on for conservatory G. amaranthus, Mignonette, zonal Geraniums, Ageratum A. lophantha. Stoped and thinned vines in late houses.

Thursday 19	Wind W. fine morning, rain in afternoon. Putting out more bedding plants in borders & filling up vacancies in beds where others had died.

Friday 20	Wind S.W. dull M. bright A. Mowed lawn all over, finished bedding out, potted off first lot of cinerarias, put in cold frame.

Saturday 21	Wind S.W. rather dull very close & warm. Potted off Centaurea & Cineraria maritima Candidissima Tansonia van Volsomi. Gathered first lot of Peas of the first crop sown the beginning of Feb^ry, variety Sancesters No 1 protected during frost.

Sunday 22	W. N.W. fine day. Went to I. church M. & E. Anthem sung at each service. Very touching & effective sermon preached in M. by Revd Stenton Eardley from Hebrews 7.25 v.

Monday 23	Wind N.W. fine not very bright. Cleared out pit where Potatoes have been growing to be ready for Cucumbers and Melons.

Tuesday 24	Wind N.W. dull few showers of rain. Cleaning up Conservatory introducing Fuschias, Hydrangeas, Ferns & Pelargoniums. Large frame filled with hot dung for Cucumbers & Melons. M^r. Y's Son buried.

Wednesday 25	Wind N.W. cloudy fine morning. Pulled weeds out from seed beds of winter greens, celery, Endive etc howed between Currants & Gooseberries.

Thursday 26	Wind N.W. fine morning, few drops of rain in middle of day, dull latter part. Howing between crops. Got in peat for potting hard wooded plants.

Friday 27	Wind N.W. very warm & bright. Potted Heaths & Epacrises keeping them indoors. Mowed lawn. Howed flower beds & borders. Watered seed beds of vegetables & celery in trenches.
Saturday 28	Wind N.W. fine day. Cleaned out potting shed, partitions put up for separating pots. Cut edges of Lawn and cleaned up. Grass cut in field for hay.
Sunday 29	Wind N.W. fine. M. very warm, heavy rain in A. & E. Went to I.C. M. A. & E. Sermons preached & collections made for Irish church Missions by Arc[dn] Townsend.
Monday 30	Wind W. dull & damp rained heavily A.& E. Cleaned plants in Early Vinery, stopped laterals of Vines. Fruit just beginning to colour. Shifted young specimen Fuschias and Celosia japonica, planted Lycopodium denticulatum & Caesia under the stage. Soil put in frames for Cucumbers & Melons.

JULY 1873

Tuesday 1	Wind W. fine day & warm. Potted off seedling Cyclamens into small 60 pots, stood them on shelf in Early Vinery. Layed runners of strawberries for forcing, in large 60s. Shook out hay in the field. Onions thinned. Planted out Cucumbers & Melons in frame.
Wednesday 2	Wind W. fine day. Stopping laterals of Vines & thinning fruit in late houses. Hay shook out & cocked up for carting.
Thursday 3	Wind S.W. rather cloudy, little rain in M. very drying wind. Thining grapes in late houses. Hay carried, stacked & raked.
Friday 4	Wind W. warm & showery at intervals. Mowed lawn all over with machine. First lot of Peas gathered from 2nd crop sown Feb[ry] 21st variety Laxtons Supreme.
Saturday 5	Wind W. showery. Cleaned up Vinerys. Cut edges of lawn round vases, trees, &c.
Sunday 6	Wind W. rather cloudy. Went to I.C. M & E had tune Hollingside in E.

Monday 7   Wind S.W. fine day & warm. Began pruning & nailing in young wood of fruit trees on walls. Ground dug for brussels sprouts.

Tuesday 8   Wind S.W. warm rather dull. Put in cuttings of yellow Allysum & Pinks in frame covered with lights & shaded.

Wednesday 9   Weather same as yesterday. Pruning and nailing on walls. Brussells sprouts planted, had ¹/₂ doz Balsams from Miss L.

Thursday 10   Wind S.W. warm rather cloudy. Coleworts pricked out. P & N fruit trees on walls.

Friday 11   Wind S. warm fine day. Mowed lawn.

Saturday 12   Wind S. rather cloudy heavy shower of rain at one o'clock. P. & N. wall trees and sweeping up.

Sunday 13   Wind S.E. rained heavily all day begining 10.30 in morning with strong wind. Went to I. Church Morning & Evening.

Monday 14   Wind S. showery. Veitch's A. Giant Cauliflower planted out and more Savoys. Potted off first lot of Primula sinensis (sown 14.5.73) into small 60s. P & N wall trees.

Tuesday 15   Wind S.W. very heavy showers of rain with thunder. B. laid up with boil on ankle. Accidents to children on pleasure vans by falling off opposite the Pied Bull Inn in the morning a boy pitching on his head died during the day, the evening a little girl whilst changing places with her sister not much hurt. Went to Rehearsal of the children of the band of hope (last time) for the great Temperance Fête at Crystal Pallace.

Wednesday 16   Wind S. lovely day. Pruned rampant shoots of standard & pyramid fruit trees. Specimen Maidenhair ferns from drawing room put in 1st vinery to recover. Accident to horse & chaise in Ellison Road; horse having his bits taken out to feed started off at a rapid pace breaking off hind wheels of chaise & jumped over a gate by which he stopped himself, no one hurt.

Thursday 17   Wind S. cloudy morning bright afternoon. Pruned std & pmd fruit trees. Ditto & nailed on walls.

Friday 18   Wind S.W. very showery. Put sticks to Peas Var. Carters Leviathan. P & N Plumbs on north wall. Fat pig fetched away by Mr. Ridnor's man.

Saturday 19   Wind S. fine day, warm. Cleaned up conservatory, brought out all Pelargoniums & Calceolarias, took in Mignonette, Amaranthus salicifolius, Achimenes, specimen Fuschias, Celosia japonica. Cut lawn.

Sunday 20   Wind W. very warm. Went to I. church M. & E. Went to Mitcham & Tooting in A. with Landlord.

Monday 21   Wind W. hot & bright. Cutting down weeds between crops. Took flowers for Mrs. Sandaver.

Tuesday 22   Wind W. fine day very warm. Went to Crystal Pallace with Lizzie & Johnny to Temperance Fête, number of visitors 53,090.

Wednesday 23 Wind N.W. very warm. Runner Beans, Peas & Tomatoes mulched with short dung. P & N Plumbs on North wall.

Thursday 24   Wind W. warm day. P & N on North wall. Trenches dug out between fruit trees for celery.

Friday 25   Wind W. fine day. Mowed lawn & cut down weeds on flower borders &c.

Saturday 26   Wind S.W. rather dull. Stopped laterals of late vines and dusted fruit with sulphur to destroy mildew. Went to London at night took watch to be mended at S. Hill.

Sunday 27   Wind S.W. very warm slight shower of rain in afternoon. Went to I. Church M. & E.

Monday 28   Wind W. very hot. Tagged down shoots of Melons & Cucumbers stopping them at same time howing between crops. Took L. & J. to singing class, Mr. Bastard conducting.

Tuesday 29   Wind W. Pruning & Nailing Peaches & Apricots on S. wall. Lizzie and Johnny left for home. Saw them start from Streatham Station.

Wednesday 30   Wind S.W. very warm sky overcast at times with heavy clouds like thunder storms. Top dressed border in cucumber house. P & N Apricots Peaches &c on walls.

Thursday 31   Wind S. cloudy greater part of day. Sowed seed of Calceolaria & Cineraria own saving. P. & N. fruit trees on walls.

AUGUST 1873

Friday 1   Wind S.W. heavy shower of rain in morning. Thining, stopping & nailing up tomatoes on walls. Celery between fruit trees planted out. Took down Stephanotis's from roof of Early Vinery & cleaned and trained on stakes.

Saturday 2   Wind S.W. fine day, warm. Mowed lawn, cut edges, swept up &c. M^r. & M^rs. Yeo left home on a visit to Wales.

Sunday 3   Fine day, cloudy at times. Went to I. church M. & E. Had tune 222 A. & M. Went to Penge in afternoon for a walk.

Monday 4   Wind S. dull indicative of rain in evening. Pruning & Nailing Peaches & Apricots. Smoked Cucumber House, allso melons in frame.

Tuesday 5   Wind S. very dull few showers during the day at Streatham. Went by excursion to Eastbourne. Weather dull in morning, no rain, fine afternoon. Went by 7.10 am. returned from Eastbourne 9.5 p.m.

Wednesday 6   Wind S.W. Finished P. & N. wall trees. Purple sprouting Brocoli & Kale planted out.

Thursday 7   Wind S. very warm. Put stakes to Phloxes, Chrysanthemums, Dahlias and other things.

Friday 8	Wind S.W. fine day, hot. Mowed lawn. Cut down weeds in borders. Watered beds and borders with hose.
Saturday 9	Wind S.W. very strong, few showers of rain. Bedding Geraniums, classed and labelled according.
Sunday 10	Wind S.W. very much like rain. Went to I.C. M. & E. Revd. Eardley unwell, unable to do duty.
Monday 11	Wind S.W. nice rain during the night, showery day. Seed sown of Spinach, Turnip & Cabbage. Cleaned up Conservatory, took in Asters, Globe Amaranthus, Celosia japonica, Mignonette.
Tuesday 12	Wind S. cloudy, no rain. Started by 5 in morning with Mr. Daniels to Norwood to see Mr. Turner, looked over the Garden, had breakfast with Mr. T., brought away cuttings of Geranium Vesuvius. Cleared up clippings of privet hedge near potting shed stood plants in front of it, brought out Azaleas from vinery also Solanums from shelf in cucumber house.
Wednesday 13	Wind S.W. very strong, rather cloudy. Took up layers of Strawberries in pits for forcing. Brought out from late vinery Geraniums for Conservatory, put out full sun to ripen wood. Gathered Morello cherries on walls.
Thursday 14	Wind S.W. fine day. Sifted cinders used ashes for bed to stand cutting of Geraniums on. Began propagating Geraniums, went over Melons and Cucumbers, thinned and stopped them, fruit of Melons just swelling off.
Friday 15	Wind S. few showers in morning, dull, bright afternoon. Fire lit in late vinerys. Stopped laterals. Mowed lawn. Layed Pinks &c for M^{r.} K—y.
Saturday 16	Wind S.W. fine, very warm. Cut edges of lawn, beds &c and cleaned up. Went to London in evening to see E.A.C.
Sunday 17	Fine day. Met E.A.C. at S.H. Station. Went to I. church M. & E. Saw E.A.C. from S.H. at night by 9.30 p.m. train.
Monday 18	Wind S. dull & showery. Had fire in late vinerys. Put in cuttings of Geraniums. Lettuces planted out.

Tuesday 19	Wind S. showery day. Rolled all walks. Putting in cuttings of Bedding Geraniums. Foresters Fête at C. Pallace. Barret went.
Wednesday 20	Wind south. Fine morning, showers in middle of day & afternoon. Went in morning by 8 a.m. train to Kings X. Went with E.A.C. to Kew Gardens, saw Gifford. Annual tea for S. school children held.
Thursday 21	Wind S.W. fine day. Putting in cuttings of bedding Geraniums, washed sulphur off vines with syringe. Sent P.O.O. for 11/- to A. Silverston 72 S.H. for mending watch.
Friday 22	Wind S.W. showery. Mowed lawn, cut edges &c. Received watch from A.S. Went over to Penge via Crystal P. Met E.A.C. went to Mr Currys.
Saturday 23	Wind S. fine day, warm. Left work at 1.30. Went by 2.49 train from S. Common to Victoria. Met E.A.C. at Balam. Went through Houses of Parliament, Westminster Abbey, C. Garden &c.
Sunday 24	Fine morning. Staying at U. Lamb's. Very heavy thunder storm in evening, rained in torrents. Went to Spurgeons Tabernacle in evening, heard very nice sermon from Matth. 7.21. Slept at coffee house. Paid 3/- for 2 nights. Miss Coulthurst died.
Monday 25	Wind S.W. fine day. Left Uncle L's at 10 a.m. E.A.C. came as far as K. X arrived at S. 12 a.m. Put in Geranium cuttings. Kail planted out against Mushroom house, also Lettuce on border.
Tuesday 26	Wind S.W. little thunder & rain. Put in cuttings of Bijou & C. Palace Gem Geraniums. Sent cuttings to Miss Lloyds.
Wednesday 27	Wind S.W. Cloudy at times indicative of thunder & storms. Finished putting in cuttings of Geraniums. Stopped & tyed down shoots of Cucumbers & Melons, smoked latter for fly, also Plants in early Vinery. Began cleaning plants in beds & borders on lawn. Quick clipped on bank in field.
Thursday 28	Wind S.W. very strong, showery. Shifted strawberries (for forcing) from large 60s in which they were struck into 32s. standing them on bed of coal ashes in full sun.

Friday 29   Wind S.W. very stormy. Sponged leaves of Camellia in Conservatory, had fire in late Vinerys. Mowed part of lawn.

Saturday 30   Wind S.W. fine day, cloudy at intervals, no rain. Finished cutting lawn, trimmed edges, swept up &c. Recieved by post from E.A.C. Necktie and Pin.

Sunday 31   Dull cloudy day, few showers. Went to I.C. M. & E., very impressive & touching sermon preached in morning from 22 of Matthew, 42 ver. by Rev^d. Eardley.

SEPTEMBER 1873

Monday 1   Wind S.W. very showery. Sponging leaves of Camellias in Conservatory, lit fire in late vinerys at night, left little air on at bottom.

Tuesday 2   Wind S.W. fine morning with sun, very heavy shower at 1.15 pm., dull and showery afternoon & evening. Cleaning plants in Conservatory. Part of Onions pulled up. Turnips & Spinach thinned.

Wednesday 3   Wind N.W. fine morning, heavy showers during the day. Cleaning plants in conservatory, got in large Camellia & Myrtle. Onions all pulled up & remainder of Celery earthed up.

Thursday 4   Wind N.W. very changeable weather. Finished cleaning plants in Conservatory, cleaned floor etc. B. went to London to D^r. Scott for liver complaint.

Friday 5   Wind N.W. no rain during the day, not much sun. Mowed Lawn. Began cleaning plants in early vinery. Lit fire in both furnaces.

Saturday 6   Wind W. fine day cloudy at times. Finished cleaning plants in early vinery. Shifted Balsams into 32s also sensitive plants into 48s, cleaned borders of cucumber house stoped & tyed down shoots of cucumbers. Spoke to M[r.] Yeo about man for extra work taking up Potatoes &c. refused. Recieved from M[r.] Sandaver new boots for every day. 14/-.

Sunday 7   Wind S.W. dull heavy rain in evening. Went to I. Church M. & E. Rev[d.] E. away, two very nice sermons preached by his brother in law M[r.] Reynolds. Singing without Organ.

Monday 8   Wind S.W. very showery. Went over vines in late houses stopping laterals & thining out the leaves. Cut down Hydrangeas and put in the cuttings, standing them out of doors in full sun.

Tuesday 9   Wind S.W. few showers. Began taking up Potatoes, took up those on bank under Fruit trees &c great many bad ones. Second crop of Turnips sown. Dung prepared for Mushrooms by wetting, turning and shaking up into a heap to ferment.

Wednesday 10   Wind S.W. fine day. Began taking up Potatoes in field, good crop, about $1/3$ bad.

Thursday 11   Wind S.W. heavy rain early in morning before 6 a.m., fine day, very drying. Finished getting up Potatoes. Shifted Primulas into 48s. Potted (into 48s) Brompton Stocks for Conservatory. Went over wall trees taking off all fore rights and stopping robust shoots. Self troubled with boils, large blind one on arm, had wax plaster put on.

Friday 12   Wind S.E. fine drying day. Made up dung for Mushroom bed after mixing with it about $1/3$ of good turfy soil. Hay from field trussed and put in loft over stable. Mowed lawn.

Saturday 13   Wind S.E. showery & cold. Went with M[r.] Yeo (in carriage) to Bulb sale at 38 King St. Covent Garden by auction by J.C. Stephens. Bought several lots of Hyacinths, Narcissus &c. Silver sand came in from Reigate.

Sunday 14   Wind S.W. very showery. Went to I. church. M. & E. sermons by Rev[d.] S. Eardley. Organist returned from holliday.

Monday 15   Wind S.W. showery. Spawned Mushroom bed, cleaned up Potatoe shed.

Tuesday 16   Wind N.W. fine day, very drying. Got in Onions & put on shelves in Potatoe house. Sowed bed of Tripoli onion. Selected Bulbs for Miss Lloyd. Dutch howed borders.

Wednesday 17   Wind S.W. dull, drying wind. Privet hedge clipped. Covered Peaches with muslin to protect from Flies, Wasps &c. Shifted Poinsettias (young plants) into 48 size pots.

Thursday 18   Wind S. beautiful clear drying day. Howing & raking on borders and between Fruit trees & bushes. Recieved message from Miss Lloyd by Gardener on obedience.

Friday 19   Wind S.W. fine morning, cloudy rest part of day. Earthed up early celery. Sowed seeds (on vine border) of Hollyhock, Honesty, Sweet William & Myosotis dissitiflora. Began potting Hyacinths. Had new pots from W. George.

Saturday 20   Fine day. Truck of coal carted in, self engaged in storing them in the cellar.

Sunday 21   Wind W. dull. Went to Immanuel church Morning and evening, sermons by Rev^d. Eardley.

Monday 22   Wind S.W. fine & warm. Potting Dutch bulbs. Mowed lawn with machine.

Tuesday 23   Wind W. fine day. Finished potting bulbs & covered them over with cinder ashes. Potted Lachenalia tricolor. Lecture by D^r. Kleide on alcohol & the French war.

Wednesday 24   Wind S.E. heavy dew in morning, fine day, dull & cloudy in evening indicative of rain. Put in cuttings of Heliotrope & variegated allysum. Cleaning beds and borders. Signed pledge of total abstinence from all intoxicating drinks.

Thursday 25   Wind W. beautiful day, very warm. Finished cleaning beds & borders. Grand Wedding of Miss Mackley at corner of Greyhound Lane.

Friday 26   Wind W. very fine & warm. Potted Primulas (recieved from M^r. Willie) into 32s, put in frame & shaded. Put in cuttings of Fuschias.

Saturday 27	Wind W. foggy morning, warm day. Cut edges of Lawn &c. Swept up etc etc. Went to London in evening recieved Watch, bought pair of light boots. Hair Albert. Hymn of praise etc.
Sunday 28	Wind N. dull. Went to I.C. M. A. & E. Stranger preached in morning, Rev^d. Eardley A. & E. Had Anthem in M. O taste & see (Goss).
Monday 29	Wind N.W. dull in morning & foggy. Putting in box edging opposite Vine border. Received notice from M^r. Y. to leave.
Tuesday 30	Wind N.W. fine day. Began gathering Apples from trees on lawn. Went up to W. L. to enquire for situation. No availe.

OCTOBER 1873

Wednesday 1	Wind W. mild rather dull. Finshed gathering Apples from trees on lawn. Went in evening to Carters & Co. Nursery, Forest Hill to enquire after situation.
Thursday 2	Wind W. fine day, warm. Putting in box edging. Smoked Cucumber house & plants in Early Vinery. Sent letter to Messrs. Carter & Co. Crystal Palace Nursery with particulars for situation etc.
Friday 3	Wind W. cloudy very close & warm. Put bottles filled with beer, sugar &c among grapes, for the destruction of Wasps, Flies &c. Cut out bad berries. Mowed part of Lawn.
Saturday 4	Wind N. dull, showery early in morning. Cleaned Conservatory, finished mowing lawn, swept up &c. Gathered Pears on lawn.
Sunday 5	Wind N. fine cloudy at times. Went to I.C. M.& E. Rev^d. Eardley absent. Sermons by Rev^d. John Bradstock (Curate).
Monday 6	Wind N.W. bright morning, dull in afternoon. Shifted young seedling Cyclamens into 48 size pots, just showing flower buds, seed sown March 24. Earthed up early celery for last time. Cabbage plants put out for spring use. Dinner party at 6.30.

Tuesday 7   Wind S. very wet & cold. Cleaned up Conservatory taking in Solanums, zonal Geraniums, Acacia lophanthas &c. Cleaned Lettuce seed. Had fire in early Vinery & Cucumber house.

Wednesday 8   Wind S.W. fine day. Put in box edging. Went over Wm. Leafe's Garden and through the houses, also went to Clarke's Nursery at Brixton Hill to enquire for situation.

Thursday 9   Wind S.W. Frost in morning bright day. Rain at night. Got in doors bedding Geraniums & Hard wooded greenhouse plants. Putting in box edging.

Friday 10   Wind S.W. dull day. Arrainging plants in greenhouse. Mowed part of lawn. Wrote letter to F. Gifford.

Saturday 11   Wind S.W. very strong, cloudy like rain. Finished cutting lawn. Cleaned bedding plants and arrainged them on stage. Left the service of Mr Yeo, also coachman.

Sunday 12   Wind S. very wet all day. Went to I.C. M. & E. Sermons by Revd Eardley.

Monday 13   Wind S. very showery. Went (in morning) to Wm. Rollisson's Nursery, Tooting. Went through houses. Saw 4 new Dracaenias not yet sent out, one very compact dark, one short leaved called Amabilis, also Aralia Veitchii, the leaves very much resembling Chloris radiata. Went in afternoon to Carters Nursery Forest Hill. Obtained lodgings &c. Saw man in search of work, gave him a 1/-. Went to singing class in evening, at Streatham.

Tuesday 14   Wind S.W. fine day. Packed up books, clothes &c. for Forest Hill. Went in evening to school to rehearsal of band of Hope & drums & fife band for concert. Boys had on uniform 1st time.

Wednesday 15   Wind S.W. little frost in morning, beautiful day. Left Streatham by 11.16 train for Forest Hill. Went to Concert in evening at Chapel. Music & reading, latter very good. Admission 1/-.

Thursday 16   Wind S.W. bright day. Began work at Messrs Carter & Co's Nursery. Cleaning inside roof of Stove, taking down & cleaning Stephanotis.

Friday 17	Foggy morning. Wind S.W. clear day. Went to London to Mr. Wade, 13 Upper Seymour St. Portman square. Cleared summer plants from boxes &c. & tyed up climbers. Posted letter to H.C.
Saturday 18	Wind S. dull. Cleaning plants in Stove washed down floor &c. Cuttings of herbaceous plants being put in.
Sunday 19	Wind S.W. very damp & showery. Went to Church in M. in A. to Penge to Mr. Currey's, came home by Rail to Forest Hill.
Monday 20	Wind S.W. very strong, showery in M. dull all day. Putting in wires & tying up Stephanotis in Stove, began cleaning lime wash off glass. Lilly of Valley being potted.
Tuesday 21	Wind N.W. showery all day with high wind. Sponging leaves of plants in Stove. Hyacinths potted for exhibition.
Wednesday 22	Wind N.W. dull, few showers. Went to London to do up Grape-Vine at Francis Day's 19.20.21 Princess Street, Stamford Street. Nr. Blackfriars Bridge. Called to see Aunt Smith. Uncle laid up with scurvy in foot and leg. Went in evening to Penny Readings at school.
Thursday 23	Wind N.W. showery. Late to work in morning lost 1 hour of time. Washing glass in Stove. First load of Tan got into bed in middle.
Friday 24	Wind N.W. very dull, showery latter part of day. Cleaning Plants in Stove, shifted Palm (Calamus elegans) into larger pot, got in more tan for bed. Tank under propagating bed repaired with cement and a coating of red & white lead & steel filings.
Saturday 25	Wind W. fine day. At work in Stove. Began laying in Gooseberries & Currants just come in by rail.
Sunday 26	Wind N.W. cold. Went in M. to Christ church, Sydenham, in A. to 1 Tree Hill from which there is a good view of the country round. Went in E. to St. Saviour's church, Brockley, heard a nice funeral sermon.

Monday 27 &
Tuesday 28

Wind N.W. Little frost at night
Laying in evergreen shrubs and Roses from John Keynes, Saulsbury
Dahlias took up and stored away

Wednesday 29
– Saturday
November 1

Wind varying from N. to S. Weather changeable. Frost at night &
sometimes rain in day. Laying in trees, Fruit trees, Evergreens &c.

NOVEMBER 1873

Sunday 2

Wind W. very dull & stormy. Started out for walk to Crystal Palace with
M^r. Mawson, got as far as Sydenham Station and obliged to return on
account of the rain. Went in evening to Christ Church, Sydenham, raining
fast at same time, small congregation.

Monday 3 –
Saturday 8

Wind varying from N. to S. weather very showery & dull not much
frost. Laying in trees &c and getting up things for orders.

Sunday 9

Wind N.W. cold and extremely wet. Went to Trinity Chapel in morning
and to temporary iron church in evening, very poor latter.

Monday 10 –
Saturday 15

Weather very changeable. First part of week wet & frost alternately,
latter part dull but no rain and drying. At work in order shed getting up
orders for fruit trees, roses, shrubs &c. Began work at 7 a.m. having
breakfast first, dinner at 12 a.m., returning at 12.45 & worked till dark.

Sunday 16

Wind N. very drying. Roads & paths clean & dry. Went to Trinity Chapel
in morning. Went for walk in afternoon with M^r. M. to Crystal Palace and
back through Penge. Called in to see M^r. Currey, latter came with us across
the fields. Went to Brockley C. in evening.

Monday 17
to
Thursday 20

Wind N.W. no rain, ground clean. At work in Order Shed, getting up
roses, fruit trees, shrubs &c. Extra fine on Thursday, sun shining brightly all
day, and very warm but rained at night. Marriage of S.C. & J.A. took place
at Christ Church C. Sent book to E.A.C. for birthday present on 21st.

Friday 21
and
Saturday 22

Wind N.W. rather strong. Leaves all – most all off decideous trees.
Out jobbing, clearing up leaves and digging borders. Paid on S. night by
M^r. Saunders.

Sunday 23 Wind N.W. dull no rain. Mr. Mawson and W.K. went to London, self went to I.C. in morning, went for walk in afternoon through Lordship Lane towards Dulwich. Went in evening to Brockly Church with G.G.

MARCH 1874

Saturday 7 Left Forest Hill for Lord Braybrook's Audley End by 2.45 p.m. train, fare 5/6, looked over houses with M^r. Bryan, H.G. Went to S. Walden in evening. Called to see Aunt Smith before leaving London.

Sunday 8 Wind S. fine, bright & warm. Looked over grounds at A.E. Went in evening to Walden church. Frost (slight) at night.

Monday 9 Wind N. cold, snow fell from 11 a.m. to 3 p.m. and again at night. Potting off bedding Geraniums, finished Lord Palmerston (number of Lord Palmerston potted off 1196) & began Cristine, potted in all 1080. First house of grapes thinned 1st time, laterals tyed down in 2 house. Temperature of 1st 75° by day 65° night, 2nd 10 degrees lower. Wrote letter to E.A.C. & H.C. Made up fires at 11 p.m. Wind strong same time 1 degree of frost.

Tuesday 10 Wind N. sun shining from 10 a.m. to 11 a.m., rest part of day dull & cold, snow fell greater part of time, 11 degrees of frost 1st in morning. Potting off Geraniums; finished Christine (1719 of Christine potted off) & began Vesuvius; number potted today 1154. Achimenes & Calaliums repotted. Peaches well syringed with engine M. & A. Made up

fires at 12 p.m. Ground covered with snow 4 inches deep, 10 degrees of frost same time. Heat in all houses & pits.

Wednesday 11 Wind N. 15° of frost 1st in morning, had been 24° since 12 o'clock previous night, continued to freeze and snow falling all day. Potted off more of Vesuvius geranium, left off on account of not having more room. Began pricking off ex seed pans into zinc trays young seedlings of Golden Pyrethum in 2nd vinery. Earliest Peaches disbudded.

Thursday 12 Wind N. 7° frost, 9° during night. Pricked off more Pyrethums. Dahlia tubers started in boxes in early vinery. Cuttings put in of Irisine, Vebena & var, Abutilon. Change in weather about midday, able to give air on all places. Thawing all afternoon & evening. Thermometer stood 34° at 11 p.m. Smoked Stove at sunset, apparatus not working well was obliged to give up before getting house full, took out tender & young Ferns.

Friday 13 Wind N. slight frost in morning (24°) very mild all day. Fresh potted bedding Geraniums, watered in 3rd vinery having stood for a few days to allow soil to dry. Eucharis amazonica repotted and put in early vinery, young plants of Dracaenias shifted into larger pots in Stove. Chrysanthemums in 54s put out into pits. Fumigated Stove with home-grown tobacco.

Saturday 14 Wind N.W. very mild. Arrainged plants (foliage) in early vinery. Boxes got ready for beans half-filled with soil and put in vinery to warm through. Shallots planted in rows 1 foot apart by 6 inches in the row, bulbs pressed into the holes & top left open, whole of bed then dusted with lime. Seed sown of Roseberry Brussell sprouts & Asiatic cauliflower in open ground covered over with netting to protect from birds.

Sunday 15 Wind N.W. very mild bright M. dull A. Put shading on Stove. Stayed in all day.

Monday 16 Wind S.W. fine morning but dull from 12 o'clock till night. Cleaning plants in Greenhouse, tyed up climbers on roof. Temporary pit for hardening off bedding plants being put up in front of late vinery. Sticks put to earliest Peas. Kidney beans (raised in pans) planted in 3 feet boxes, a row on each side, 12 in a row, boxes half full of soil to allow for earthing up as they advance, shaded from sun.

Tuesday 17 Wind S. warm and showery. Tying out & arrainging plants in Greenhouse. Cut down old plant of Myrtle, took out Camellias done blooming & put in heat for early flowering. Late vines tyed up to rafters. Polemoniums, Centaureas &c put in open pit (covered at night) to make room for potting off other bedding plants more tender.

Wednesday 18 Wind S.W. showery morning up till 12 o'clock afternoon & evening clear fine & warm. Staking hard wooded plants in Greenhouses. Packed up in hamper several doz. variegated Polemoniums which were sent away by Rail. Began syringing late vines at shutting up time. Fruit stoned in 1ˢᵗ vinery, just showing in 2ⁿᵈ, eyes just starting in 3ʳᵈ. Earliest Peaches now stoning.

Thursday 19 Wind S.W. fine & drying. Cuttings put in of Heliotrope, Ageratum, Bouvardia, Euphorbia jacquiniflora &c. Bed sown of Early Store Turnip, covered with netting to keep off birds.

Friday 20 Wind N.W. Put specimen azaleas into open shed shaded from sun to keep back. Early Dalmahoy potatoes planted ceased to syringe vines in 3rd vinery & began sprinkling the walls & floor twice a day, or more if necessary. Old Fuschias started in pit.

Saturday 21 Wind N.W. very mild. Mr B. absent in morning. Mr Knuckund called. Bed of Lettuce seed sown. Shifted plants of Pteris tremula into 24s to grow on for cutting. Potted off cuttings of Allamanda & Sanchezia nobilis also seedlings of Solanum hybridum.

Sunday 22 Wind N.W. mild, fine, bright morning, cloudy, with rain at midday, continued damp rest part of day. Self on duty for first time.

Monday 23 Wind N.W. close & very warm, bright all day, thermometer 64° in shade. Stove, Early Vinery, ditto Peach house 90° during day, left a chink of air on all night. Shifted sweet scented Geraniums into 48s to grow on for cutting with flowers &c, put in late Peach house, house well smoked at night, blossoms just setting.

Tuesday 24 Wind N.W. dull, sharp wind, bright for few hours at midday. First lot of forced strawberries gathered. Bedding Geraniums (potted off 10ᵗʰ) put out into open pits to harden off, covered at night. Potted off cuttings of Deutzia gracilis, Solanums, Torenia asiatica in Stove. Autumn sown onions planted out at proper distances & watered. Mr. B. out. Well syringed Peach trees in late house to clear them of bloom where the fruit has set.

Wednesday 25 Wind N.E. slight frost in morning viz. 2° degrees, cold air all day, dull in morning, sun coming out at 10.30 & continuing bright all day. Began potting off first lot of Verbenas, 3 in small 60s. Took young plants of fuschias (in 48s from 2nd vinery into late Peach house), where they are to be grown.

Thursday 26 Wind N.W. 8 degrees of frost in morning. Potting of Verbenas. Hardy brown Cos Lettuce planted out. P. Golden Feather put in pit to harden off.

Friday 27 Wind S. blowing freely, very mild 64° in shade. Cuttings of Alternanthera put in pans in heat. Potting off bedding Geraniums. Fig trees on walls uncovered & nailed out having been tyed up & bound with hay bands all winter. Mr. B. out.

Saturday 28 Wind S. fine & warm. Cleaning & rearrainging plants in houses. Old Asparagus beds from which plants had been taken for forcing well manured, trenched and replanted with 1 year old plants of Connovers Colossal asparagus. Boat race between University of Oxford & Cambridge took place on the Thames, won by the latter.

Sunday 29 Wind S.W. very high, rather showery, changeable. Went in morning to church at Littlebury high church, surpliced choir singing very bad, went in evening to Walden church, liked service much.

Monday 30 Wind S.W. changeable, mild. Finished potting off Geraniums in tins, boxes &c in Vinery, began those in large pots, in Orchard house. J. Bedgegood sent away Geraniums by post to Ireland. Put stakes to support Hyacinths (3 to each) for exhibition. J. Bryan still away. Killed rat in garden when going to attend to fires &c at 9.30 p.m.

Tuesday 31 Wind N.W. dull, showery, and very changeable. Finished potting off all Geraniums for bedding & began to pot off Lobelias &c. Late Peaches disbudded. Fruit trees in Orchard house syringed & dusted with snuff tobacco powder &c to kill flies. Mr. B. home again. Gathered violets early in morning. Earthed up beans in boxes in 2nd vinery, planted on the 16th. Received from Mr. Bryan, wages for 3 weeks & 2 days at rate of 16/- per week. Viz £2-16-0.

APRIL 1874

Wednesday 1 Wind N.W., very changeable. Potted off Lobelias into small 60s, put in 2nd vinery. Cannas started. Shoots tyed in on trees in early Peach house. Azaleas took out from late vinery & put in Orchard house, & some in greenhouse.

Thursday 2 Wind S.W. very strong, cloudy greater part of day. Shading material on Stove torn by wind. Lachenalias (tricolor) now in full bloom, taken from pits & put in greenhouse. Put in Fuchsia cuttings, in 48s, in Stove. Cauliflower & Celery plts pricked out in boxes & put in Orchard h.

Friday 3 Wind W. in morning (changing towards evening to S.W.) bright morning, cloudy at times during the day, showery in afternoon, slight thunder storm with hail at 3 p.m. Clear & indicative of frost at night. Good Friday. Self on duty, had great deal of watering to do in morning. Mr. B. finished tying early Peaches 1st in morning.

Saturday 4 Wind S.W. fine day, rain in evening. Old plants of Alternantheras & Caladiums which were not wanted, thrown away. First bach of Verbenas (potted off) put in late Vinery to harden off. Cuttings put in of Euphorbia jacquiniflora, Echevera metallica & Centaurea raguisina compacta. Went home by 7.30 p.m. train from A.E. arrived at Cam^{bge} 8.20, walked to Grantchester in 50 minutes, very wet night.

Sunday 5 Wind S.W. dull & cloudy in the morning clearing off at 10 a.m. fine rest of day. Went to church M. & E. at the V. in afternoon. M.A.A. & Uncle J. came over to G.– r. Called on Revd. F. G. Howard in evening.

Monday 6 Wind S.W. Fine morning, little rain during day. Left home for Audley End by 1st train from Cam – viz. 7.15am. Henry came with me to station. Called to see Lizzie at 22 Trumpington St. Arrived at A. E. 7.55. Potted off Coleus for pot culture, in Stove. Covering material which has been on vine border all winter, removed, consisting of short litter, tarpaulin &c. Received from Mr. Bryan, knives and forks, tablespoons, quart saucepan &c. Mr. Butcher from London gave beer to men.

Tuesday 7 Wind S.W. Fine day, mild. Potted off Verbenas and put in early Vinery till rooted. Dahlia's which have been started thickly in zinc trays, parted up and potted. Smoked Stove at night with tobacco paper. Paid 1st bill for bread, grocery &c. 12/8¾d.

Wednesday 8   Wind N. Fine, bright & warm. Potting off Verbena's. Smoking apparatus opened & cleaned out & otherwise rectified. Smoked Stove with it at night. Work first rate. Seeds sown (out of doors) of Savoy cabbage, brocoli, kail &c. Potted off into small 60s seedling Centaurea's (gymnocarpa, Clementii) & Solanums also into large 60s var Solanums, Salvias &c.
Roses (Marechal Niel & Gloiry de Dijon) cut, first lot this year. Azalea's put into heat to forward for exhibition on the 23rd at Cambridge.

Thursday 9   Wind S. Fine morning, slight frost, cloudy towards midday, afternoon & evening windy and stormy. Chrysanthemums shifted into larger pots. Potting off Heliotropes and Abutilon thompsonii into small 60s.

Friday 10   Wind S. Very mild, damp, showery, but beautiful growing day. All seed beds dusted over with lime for destruction of slugs, fly &c. Shifted herbaceous calceolarias into 24s & 32s, removed from early vinery to Stove large Diffenbachia & Cyanophyllum, small specimen of latter shifted into larger pot also Gardeneas &c. Earliest grapes just beginning to colour, temperature at night a little lower than formerly viz. 65°. Ventilator of Orchard house stuffed with moss and well smoked for black fly. Sent letters to T Smith Perry Hill and Miss Wood, Sturry.

Saturday 11   Wind N. Dull, showery, very changeable. Went through houses putting plants in order &c. Houses cleaned up &c. 10 boxes filled with soil for beans and put in 3rd vinery. Well smoked Orchard and late Peach houses at night. Received from Mr. Bryan 1/- for extra work &c.

Sunday 12   1st Sunday after Easter, weather very dull and cloudy. Self on duty.

Monday 13   Wind S.E. Bright morning, cloudy with rain afterwards viz. 1.30 p.m. then gradually cleared off, fine afternoon. Got in Fuschias cuttings. Potted of Ageratums & put in early vinery. Beans planted in boxes in 3rd Vinery, allowed to stand on floor till recovered, so as to be a little shaded in case of sun shining. Pelargoniums put in late Peach house & well smoked, early peaches tyed down & thinned. All trees in Orchard house well syringed, shut up early with sun heat.

Tuesday 14

Wind W. dull morning, fine afternoon. Dracaena's and other plants from early Vinery plunged in tan beds in 2nd vinery, top of Cordyline Banksii cut of and inserted. More soil added to Cucumbers in frame & pegged down. Put in cuttings and leaves of various sorts of begonia's. Wind rough at night.

Wednesday 15

Wind N. Dull & cold. Potted off 3 in a large 60 P. Golden Feather. Maidenhair ferns just starting into growth, fresh potted and put in 2nd vinery. Fire engine brought out and worked for trial.

Thursday 16

Wind N. changeable, bright afternoon. M. Flowering plants got up and packed to be sent to Right Honble. Lord Brabrook, Dover St, Piccadilly. Stephanotis at end of Stove, cleaned. Began potting off Iresine Lindenii and put in Early Peach house. Specimen copy of Floral World given to J.B. by M^r. B.

Friday 17

Wind N.W. Fine day, cloudy at times, mild, thermometer standing at 50° in shade. Finished potting off Iresine. Calceolarias taken from pit in which they were struck and planted out in flower beds for the season, also, var Polemonium. Glass at end of 2nd vinery and sides of Stove whitewashed for shading.

Saturday 18

Wind N.W. Warm showery morning, showery & sunny alternately, throughout the day. Cleaning up houses, removed large Coranillas from green house, which had done blooming, to Orchard house. Put Alocasias, Bougainvillia and other plants from early Vinery and put in Stove. Seeds sown of Primula, Balsam and Clianthus dampierii put in Stove. At work later, getting down Ageratum and Heliotropes fom Early Vinery into 3rd box. Received 6d from M^r. Bryan for extra work after 6 p.m.

Sunday 19

Wind W. Very mild, thermometer 63° in shade at midday, beautiful day. Went to Walden Church morning & evening liked both services very much, went after evening service for walk through Walden towards Littlebury.

Monday 20

Wind W. Bright and warm. Self watering & syringing nearly all day, Centaurea ragusina planted out in flower beds. Red Beet sown in drills, also Ridge cucumber & Vegetable Marrow in pans in doors. Sat up till late writing letters &c to T. Mawson, M^r. Stenger and E.A.C.

Tuesday 21 Wind S. bright & clear all day, very warm thermometer 75° in shade. Opened houses early, began to shift first batch of young Fuschia's from 48s into 24s, put on stage in late Peach house. Began the watering in afternoon in pits &c. M^r. Collis at the lodge left, James Richardson in the house for a time.

Wednesday 22 Wind E. Bright, warm day, cloudy at evening. Potting Fuchsias into 24s. Plants got ready & packed for Exhibition at Cambridge, 4 Azaleas (3 & 1) Tulips, Hyacinths, Primroses, & 3 plants in bloom, viz Anthurium Scherzerianum, Eucharis Amazonica & 1 Azalea. Cuckoo & Nightingale first heard.

Thursday 23 Wind S.E. bright & warm all day. Potted off Heliotropes. Shifted 2 plants of Araucaria excelsa into larger pots in greenhouse. Trees on walls dusted with tobacco powder for fly &c. Horticultural show at Cambridge, received 1st prize for Azaleas Hyacinths, Primroses and 3 plants in bloom, 2nd for best plant.

Friday 24 Wind S. cloudy morning, warm day but not very bright. Shook out & repotted old plants of Fuchsia's, also young grafted Roses into 32s. Bed of ashes made up outdoors for golden feather & other things from pits. Verbenas planted out in frame, gathered 1st crop of beans in 2nd vinery, planted in boxes March 16th. Young colt at farm castrated, cut first brace of cucumbers in frame. Figs stoped and thinned out in late Peach house, laterals of S's thinned also.

Saturday 25 Wind S. bright morning, but rather dull rest part of day. Cleaning up and rearanging plants in all houses. Celery (raised indoors & hardened off) pricked out in beds in open ground.

Sunday 26 Wind S.E. bright & very warm day. Self on duty, had great deal watering to do. J. Bedgegood went to Chesterford Park. Captn. Elliott's to look over garden &c. Brought home 2 cuttings of G. Jean Sisley.

April — 1874

S 19 Wind W very mild, thermometer 63° in shade
at midday, beautiful day, Went to
Walden Church morning & evening
liked both services very much, went
after evening service for walk through
Walden towards Littlebury

M 20 Wind W bright & warm, self watering & syringing nearly all day
Centaurea ragusina planted out
in flower beds. Red Beet sown
in drills, also Ridge Cucumber & Vegetable Marrow in pans in doors
Sat up till late writing letters &c.
to T. Mawson. Mr Stenger and E.A.C.

T 21 Wind S. bright & clear all day, very warm
thermometer 75° in shade, opened houses
early, began to shift first batch of

W 22 Wind E. bright warm day, Cloudy ah eveni
Potting Fuchsias into 24s, Plants got
ready & packed for Exhibition ah
Cambridge, 4 Azaleas 3+1) Tulips,
Hyacinths, Primroses, & 3 plants in
bloom, viz Anthurium Scherremania
Eucharis Amazonica, + 1 Azalea
Cuckoo & Nightingale first heard

J 23 Wind S.E. bright & warm all day
potted off Heliotropes. Shifted
2 plants of Araucaria excelsa in
to larger pots in green house,
Trees on walls dusted with tobacco
powder for fly &c Horticultural
show ah Cambridge, received
1st prize for Azalea's Hyacinths, Primroses
and 3 plants in bloom, 2nd for best plant

Monday 27	Wind S.E. beautiful day. Cleaned up Orchard house. Greenhouse and part of Stove whitewashed to afford shading to plants inside. Earthed up beans in 3rd vinery which were planted on the 13th.
Tuesday 28	Wind S.E. fine day. Put glasses to some of cucumbers, gave whole a good watering. Vines in 3rd vinery just in bloom.
Wednesday 29	Wind S.E. slight frost, bright all day but not very warm. Potted of cannas that have been started in box. Beans sown in 24 pots, put in late vinery. Saw for the 1st time this year a Martin or Swallow.
Thursday 30	Wind N. 4° of frost in morning, not done much damage; bright & warm all day. Seeds sown out of doors of Zinnia's, Stocks, Asters & other annuals. Shifted young Pelargoniums into 48s, in pit. Sprinkled at Midday, Vinerys & Peach houses with liquid manure, as being beneficial to them, by giving off a quantity of ammonia. Received of Mr. Bryan for month's wages or 4 wks & 2 dys £3-9-4. Sale of plts at Southgate yesterday & today.

MAY 1874

Friday 1	Wind N.E. Cold and dull at times. Little sun. Shifted young Coleus's into 48 size pot and put in pit. Potted 2nd batch of Achimenes into 48 and 32 size pots stood on sand over flue in Stove. Large fire at Radwinter, farm and 24 cottages burnt down. Fire engine went from Ld Brabooks.
Saturday 2	Wind N.E. rather dull, clouds indicative of storms, little fall of hail. Cleaning up and rearainging plants in houses, inferior sorts of Auriculars and Poleanthus thrown away. Zinc trays (sown with Tagetes signata pumila just up), removed from 1st to 3rd vinery. At work till 1/2 past seven watering &c. Cold at night.
Sunday 3	Wind N.E. Very cold & showery, with hail. Went for walk in morning to Walden via A.E. Stayed in rest of day.
Monday 4	Wind N.E. changeable in morning, dull all afternoon & evening. Shifted Gloxinia's into larger pots pinching off all bloom buds, to come on later, potted off Alternantheras & Coleus (splendens). Czar violets in pots divided into single crowns and planted out in border of rich soil a foot apart.

Tuesday 5	Wind N.E. very changeable, not much sun. Potted off young plants of Dracaena Cooperi and Bouvardias & Balsams. Shifted into larger pots Difenbachia's, Caladium's, Dracaena's, Allamanda's, Sanchezia nobilis & other things in Stove. Put in cuttings of Coleus for 2nd batch. Seeds sown in kitchen garden of Brocoli, Kail, Cabbages & other greens.
Wednesday 6	Wind N.E, changing to S in afternoon, fine, cloudy at times. Shaking out and repotting old plants of Geraniums and potting others off. Shifted also into 32s Sparrmannia africana. Smoked Pelargoniums in pit in the evening.
Thursday 7	Wind S., changing at midday to N. Weather changeable. Potting up Geraniums for pot culture. Strawberries well watered with liquid manure, also fruit trees newly planted, with clean water, which are mulched with short dung.
Friday 8	Wind N.W, rather stormy. Finished potting old plants of Geraniums in pits. Smoked Pelargoniums in pit. Grapes in late vinery in bloom, temperature 75° at night, 80° or more by day with sun heat. Strawberries that have been watered, mulched with clean straw to preserve the fruit from dirt.
Saturday 9	Wind N.W. dull and cloudy greater part of day, with storms. Cleaning plants in houses and putting them in order.
Sunday 10	Wind N.W. dull and cold, few showers. Self on duty, deal of watering to do. Began two of us getting up first in morning to get principal work done early.
Monday 11	Wind N.E. Very cold, 5° of frost this morning and yesterday morning. Earthed up beans in pots (3 in a 24 size) and put on shelf in late vinery, grapes in this house now in bloom, atmosphere kept dryer with more heat viz 75° by night, 85° by day or more with sun heat, these are Muscats. First lot cut from early houses, Lady Braybrook came on a visit for the day accompanied by the chaplain.
Tuesday 12	Wind N.E. 5° of frost in morning, dull greater part of day, no rain. Fresh potted plants of Crotons, Accalypha and Hybiscus Cooperii. Put in cuttings of Panicum, 3 in a small 60 size pot. Mr. Bryan away till evening,

self gathered strawberries which were sent to London in the evening with flowers &c. Trenches dug out for celery, 1 foot ½ wide by 2½ feet between each trench. Trees in Orchard house (in pots) well mulched with good rotten dung to which had been added a small quantity of guano.

Wednesday 13   Wind N.E. in morning & all day, changing in evening to S. dull all day but mild. Fruit trees on walls disbudded. French Beans raised in boxes, planted out & covered at night with mats to protect from frost. Potatoes are now black from frost, late fruit also injured.

Thursday 14   Wind N. dull all day, mild. Syringing Pelargoniums in pit that have been smoked to clean them from dead flies and dirt. Grapes thinned in 3 vinery 1st time. Muscats in late house now setting. Woodwork & blinds on walls over Apricots taken down & stored away. First heard of Mr. Young's leaving. Gentle rain at night.

Friday 15   Wind S. 1st in morning bright & clear, changing at 7.30 a.m. to N.W., when a storm arose, rained heavily for a short time, continued to be stormy all the morning, but fine afternoon. Fresh potted, and shifted that required it, Camellia's that have made their new groth putting them in pit kept close & shaded from bright sun. Cord on light in green house broke in evening; put new one to it. Shifted into larger pots specimen of Croton Pictum, soil peat loam (equal parts) l. mould.

Saturday 16   Wind N.W. 3° of frost, bright morn, fine day though cloudy at times. Put pot vines on large pots to bring them close to the glass. Cleaning houses &c. Syringed all houses at shutting up time.

Sunday 17   Wind N.W. bright morning, 5° of frost, warm day. Went to Walden Church M. & E. Littlebury in A. Went up to aviary in afternoon, Saw pheasants &c. Received by post 3 books and 1 letter in print on 'Nervous Debility'.

Monday 18   Wind N.W. dull morning, 6° of frost, cloudy greater part of day. Getting up plants for May Open show at Cambridge on 20th, cleaning them &c. Self broke large pot in which was specimen of Lomaria gibba. Trees in Orchard house being disbudded, fruit thinned etc. Fruit trees borders out-doors dressed with dung from Mushroom bed about 2 ft wide from wall & forked up.

Tuesday 19 Wind N., mild, not much sun. Getting up plants for Exhibition by sponging, tying out, etc, all packed in Bullock cart & stood out doors all night no protection besides tilth. Fruit trees in Orchard house disbudded etc, long groths cut back to $^1/_3$ on Apricots, plums & cherries.

Wednesday 20 Wind N.E. no sun all day, warm and close, clouds indicative of rain. Horticultural show at Cambridge in fellows grounds Kings Coll. Van (or cart) started at 5 a.m. Self watering till 12 a.m. then put President strawberries in late Peach house, top dressed large specimen white Azalea. Potted off 2nd batch of Coleus & put on front slab in 3rd vinery. Seed beds in kitchen garden well watered; slipped in tank in 2nd vinery, tore trousers. Cut Cucumbers for Mr. Warren. For plants exhibited at Cambridge recieved 1st prize for Amarillis, 2nd & 3rd for Foliage plants, 2nd for 1 Azalea, extras for coll. Dracaenias & Grapes.

Thursday 21 Wind N.E. mild, fine day. Unloaded plants from cart which were exhibited and aranged them in houses, large Difenbachia put in late Vinery, shifted into 16 size pot Sphaerogene latifolia. Water pipes round houses repaired.

Friday 22 Wind N.E. very warm, 80° out-doors in shade. Old plants of Geraniums planted out in mixed beds. Put in cuttings of Begonia's & Tradescantia discolour in 48s pots in Stove. Gave grapes in late Vinery (Muscats) good syringing to clear them of old blossoms, calyx etc. Strawberries forced & hardened off, planted out in rows yard apart. Annuals well watered. All bedding plants exposed all night, few peals of thunder at 5.50 p.m. rather cloudy same time but no rain.

Saturday 23 Wind N.E. dull morning, very mild, rain began falling between 7 & 8 o'clock & continued to fall nearly all day. Chrysanthemums shifted into 9 & 11 inch pots, left in shed till Monday. Took Caladiums from 2nd to 3rd Vinery. Herbaceous Calceolarias in bloom, put some in Greenhouse. More Seeds sown of Veitch's Autumn Giant Cauliflowers in Kitchen Garden.

Sunday 24 Wind S.E. no rain dull but mild. Self on duty, very little work to be done, little sun mid-day & early afternoon.

Monday 25 Wind S.E. dull & close, Thunder about with gentle showers. Took out chrysanthemums which were potted on Sat. & put in lower slip on bed of ashes. Potted off 2nd batch into large 60s in pit, Ridge cucumbers, Vegetable Marrows & Tomatoes planted out, protected with hand-lights. Onions thinned 1st time. Several visitors round with Mr. Bryan. J.B. recieved from them perquisite's 4/-, 1st dish of early Peas gathered. Solanums and Alosia's planted out on Peach border.

Tuesday 26   Wind S.E. fine & bright, very warm. Began putting out bedding plants, Geraniums &c. Packed up basket of plants in bloom for London to Lord Braybrook. Miss Whitehead (formerly cook at Revd. A. D. Capels) called in evening to see me. Received letter from H.C. with vignette photo.

Wednesday 27   Wind S.E. bright & very warm. Verbenas planted out in beds. Potted Gesneria's singly in large 60s, started in stove with bottom heat to be shifted on as required. Put in cuttings of Pelargoniums (early) varieties Snowdrop & Gauntlet. Capsicums potted off & put in Cucumber frame till rooted.

Thursday 28 Wind S. very warm, plenty of air, not much sun, clouds indicative of storms. Geraniums (Vesuvius & Bayard) put out. Shifted young plts of Echevera retusa sinensis into 32s for winter blooming. Repotted large Camellia's in Green-house. Ceased syringing earliest peaches which are now nearly ripe. Cherry tree in Orchard house pulled up, having failed. Cherries outdoors on walls covered with netting to keep off birds.

Friday 29 Wind S. mild, cloudy, drying. Mangle's Geranium planted out, also variegated Abutilon. Potted off young Fuschias into small 60s & put on front slab in 3rd vinery. J.B. sent away. Young Fuschias and Geranium Vesuvius with Double Lobelias. First basket of peas taken.

Saturday 30 Wind S. very mild, not much sun. Shifted Salvia splendens into 32s & put in pit. Went home by 7.30 p.m. train, got off at Shelford, arrived at Grantchester about 9.

Sunday 31 Wind S., lovely day, plenty of air. Rose in morning before 5 o'clock, went for a walk with H. & F. towards Haslingfield. Went to chch M. A. & E. Mrs. Carlton & M.A.A. came over in evening. Myself & E.A.C. went part of way back with them. Photos of Lizzie came by post. Swarm of Bees taken at Lord Braybrooks.

JUNE 1874

Monday 1 Wind S., mild, changeable. Left G. for A. End by 7.15 train ex Cambridge, took leave of Lizzie, who going into place on Wed. in Sussex with Ester Pope. H. came with me to C. stn, arrived at A.E. 8 o'clock. Large quantity of fruit & vegetables sent to Lord Braybrooks for party. Bedding plants put out at Lodge near stables. Potted off Tagetes signata pumila. Swarm of bees hived.

Tuesday 2 Wind S. very close & warm & bright, Thunder in afternoon with heavy shower of rain. Potting of Tagetes signata pumila. W^m. Claydon stung by bees whilst swarming, on eye, swelled very much. Mr. B. went to London by mail train (mid-day). Catching Bats in evening with net, as they flew out from corner of room. Sat up late writing letters to Aunts Mary & Amy and M^r. Kennedy.

Wednesday 3   Wind S. mild. Cut flowers in morning for table bouquet. Mr Bryan came home at mid-day. Potting off Tagetes and shifted Tree Carnations, then began to clean Green house for painting. Nest of jackdaws taken, side of river, Moule had one.

Thursday 4   Wind S. very bright, hot & drying. Ageratums planted out. Shifted Balsams into 32s. Threw away last of Cineraria's. Went to Walden in evening. Saw Volunteers on Common. Ceased to have fire in Stove.

Friday 5   Wind S. beautiful day, 75° in shade. Put Nets over Cherries in Orchard house. Hamper of zonal Geraniums in 32s sent to Walden. Coals being got in for House. Men from kitchen garden helping.

Saturday 6   Wind S. bright & hot 1st half of day, latter part cloudy & stormy with thunder, nice rain late in evening. Lord & Lady Braybrook & family came home for purpose of attending Littlebury church on the 9th on the occasion of consecration of new chancel. All houses cleaned up. Green house made gay as possible, at work till dark watering etc.

Sunday 7   Wind S. mild mor^{ng}, but dull, clearing up about mid-day, warm, bright afternoon not very drying so had not much watering to do. James Bedgegood went to Wenden church in A.

Monday 8   Wind S. fine morning, bright & hot all day. Shaded pits to prevent over drying. Beans (planted in boxes in 3rd vinery April 13th) now last lot picked & thrown away. Plants got ready and took to Littlebury church. Mr. B. went out in evening with cart took Bedding plants, came home 10.30 p.m.

Tuesday 9   Wind S. bright & cloudless, very warm. Potted off 1st batch of Primulas and Cinerarias. Double Primulas divided & fresh potted in peat & sand. 2nd batch of Balsam sown. 6 doz Alternanthera magnifica came in. New chancel of Littlebury church opened by the Lord Bishop of Rochester, 3 services.

Wednesday 10   Wind S.W. bright morning, afterwards cloudy, dull & cold. Potted off Cyclamen persicum into small 60s stood on front slab in 3rd vinery. 3 lights of Melons planted in frame (or pit). British & other Ferns repotted in pits. Potted of last batch of Fuschia. New Stools put down for bee hives to rest upon.

Thursday 11   Wind S. blowing rather strongly all day, changing in evening to N.W., very bright and hot in morning dull afternoon. Thermometer been down to 33° overnight. Shifted Capsicums into 48s standing them in pit. Bedding plants put out in Fishpond ground. Cut down last of Pelargonium Gauntlet & put in cuttings. Called in late vinery at night or evening by M^r. Bryan to water beans in pots.

Friday 12   Wind N.E. very cold all day, cloudy at times. Iresine & Heliotropes planted out in Flower garden. Shifted Achimenes into larger pots. Staked Croton pictum. 1st lot of Strawberries layed in 48 pots for forcing var. Black Prince.

Saturday 13   Wind N.E. Thermometer last night registered 2 deg. of frost. Bedding plants nipped that are put out; also Potatoes. Up early to gather Strawberries to be sent with other fruit to London by 1st train. Part of Maidenhair ferns put in pit to harden for cutting.

Sunday 14   Wind N. cloudy & sun shining alternately throughout the day, some heavy clouds in M. with few drops of small rain. At work till breakfast watering etc. Went to Walden church M. & E. to Littlebury in A. when the sermon was preached by Rev Latimer Neville; stayed after service to look at chancel. In the evening at Walden Rev^d. Beasley preached his farewell sermon to a large congregation from 2nd chap of Collossians 5th, 6th & 7th verses. Hallelujah Chorus played as a Voluntary after the service.

Monday 15   Wind N. very drying day, dull in evening & cold. Posted 4 Newspapers to E.A.C., H.C., F.H.S., & Miss W. (Sturry). Peas in kitchen garden well watered. Shifted Chrysanthemums (for cut flowers for Exhibition) into 16 & 24 size pots. Plants fetched home from Littlebury church. Raining (very fine) late in evening viz. at 9 p.m.

Tuesday 16   Wind N.E. cold, not much sun, dull all A., rained heavyly at 9 & 10 p.m. Shifted Geraniums Vesuvius & Master Christine, also Centaurea gymnocarpa into 48 and 32 size pots, put in open pit. Watered front of border (inside) in late vinery. Staked largest plant of Adiantum Farleyense. M^r. B. away.

Wednesday 17   Wind N. raining heavily 1st in morning had been raining all night, cleared off at 11 a.m., little sun then till 2.30 p.m. dull afternoon. Parting up & repotting Selaginella denticulata & Isolepis gracilis in Stove. Threw away old plants of Pariensis replaced with fresh struck ones. Strawberries which failed all turned out (variety President). Boy came in garden for frightening birds from fruit. Bees swarmed. M^r. B. out in evening with cart.

Thursday 18   Wind N. very mild, cloudy all day, no sun, up at 5 a.m. to look after fires which were allowed to get low last night. Plants in Stove being cleaned, Dracaenas all sponged, shifted some into larger pots, also Alocasia lowii, Euphorbia jacquiniflora and smallest plant of Adiantum farleyense. Potted young seedling (spontaneous) Ferns. Put mats under Peaches over hotwater pipes to catch fruit, threw away useless specimen of Lemaria Gibba. Took plant stand up to house, having been fresh painted.

Friday 19   Wind N. dull all mor., bright in afternoon. Cleaning & arranging plants in Stove. M^r. Bryan went off by first train, returned again at night.

Saturday 20   Wind N. dull & close all day. Finished arranging plants in Stove. Cleaned up other houses etc. Maranta Vietchii and Cyanophyllum magnificum removed from tan bed in 2nd vinery to Stove. Cuttings put in of Cyanophyllum and Sphaerogyne in Stove. Went to Walden at night.

Sunday 21   Wind S.E. very bright morning, fine all day. Self on duty.

Monday 22   Wind S.E. bright 1st in morning, slightly overcast at 7 a.m. cloudy at times (but very warm) till 1.30. dull afternoon. Poinsettia pulcherima brought out from back of Greenhouse, cleaned up, put on slab in front of 3rd vinery, well watered to start for cuttings. Shifted last batch of Chrysanthemums into 32 size pots. Tagetes signata put out in beds in flr. garden. Moule's Pig loose in Nursery.

Tuesday 23   Wind S. very changeable. Plants all got together in late vinery, sponged & pots washed etc. for exhibition at Walden. Strawberry runners layed (var. Reens seedling) in 32 size pots as an experiment they having been filled with good soil and made firm. Sat up late at night mending Trousers and coat.

Wednesday 24   Wind S.W. rained heavily early in morning, showery all day, very heavy shower at 9.30 a.m. with hail, fine evening. Flower Show at Walden took van load of plants (foliage) put out not for competition, received special prize. Show altogether very good. R. Ardneth & friend called to see me, also B. Fred & A. Unwin. Showed them through houses and over garden etc, 2 latter stayed to dinner with me, saw all from Audley End station at night. Band of Royal Artillery at Show sang several pieces, saw Mr. G. Webb.

Thursday 25   Wind S. fine day few light showers. Fetched home & placed plants from W. show. Horticultural show at Cambridge. Mr. Bryan went by Rail. Useless Strawberries taken up, ground well manured & dug up, trod firm and planted with Savoys. Kail of sorts planted out for Winter use.

Friday 26   Wind S. mild, dull, few showers throughout the day. Took Fuschias from late Peach house & put in pits. Seedling Cinerarias & Primula's in small 60s sorted through took out from pits & put in 2 light box under north wall. Walden Rifle Volunteers drilled in evening in Deer Park, appeared for 1st time in new uniform (red coats, black trousers, white belts); went up to

see them, late Peaches thinned (last time). Seed sown of Brompton Stock in open ground.

Saturday 27

Wind S.E. dull early in morning, cleared up 10.45 a.m. bright and warm rest part of day. Cleaning up houses, etc. Temporary stage of boards, etc, at back of late Peach House took out & stored away. Cherries in pots (fruit ripe) in Orchard house removed to early Vinery. Annual ringing of bells at Walden Church. Garden woman forgot to bring clean linen.

Sunday 28

Wind N.E. mild, very changeable, few light showers in morning, very warm & bright at shutting up time. Brother H. came, went to meet him, came back & shelled green Peas, being 1st time having them. Went to Littlebury Church in Aftern and in evening to Walden. Sermon preached at latter for Missionary S. Hallelujah Chorus played for Voluntary after service (not Handel's). H^ry went home by mail train ex Audley E.

Monday 29

Wind S.E. bright clear morning becoming cloudy at midday with rain, continued dull rest of day. Shifted 3 pot Vines in Orchard h^se. into larger pots for forcing next year. Trees in Orchard house gone over & young wood pruned back. Put in cuttings of Centaurea ragusina etc. Box of honey taken from bees at midday by M^r. Bryan.

Tuesday 30

Wind S.W. beautiful fine day, and very warm. Took out from late Peach house Scented Geraniums and shifted them into 32s standing them in pit to come on for cutting. Coleus & young Fuschia's taken ex front slab in 3rd vinery & put in pit. E.A.C.. M.A.A., & E.G. came to look over the place, arriving at 11.45 a.m. went with them to Aviary & through house, etc. also to station in evening, too late for 7.30 train had to wait for mail at 10.45 p.m. Had tea with me. E.A.C. brought clothes for me from home which had been mended. Rec^d. Ex Mr. Bryan £3.9.4. for 1 month's wages. Threw open early Peach house.

JULY 1874

Wednesday 1

Wind S.W. dull all day, showery in morning. J. Bedgegood went by early train to show at Stratford. Potted off 2nd batch of Balsams. Put in cuttings of Coprosma Baureana. Filled large Fern Case. Leeks planted out. Watered Strawberry runners in evening.

Tuesday 2

Wind S.W. beautiful bright morning, overcast at breakfast time with few showers; cleared off at 10.30, very hot rest of day, Thermometer 86° in shade. Water in river let off, cascade under repairs. Stood Fruit trees in pots in Orchard house on bricks, to allow water to pass off freely. Trees dusted with Tobacco powder to kill flys. Part off roof of late vinery (over Lady Downes) whitewashed to prevent scalding or scorching. Filled large hanging basket with flowering plants (bedding and trailing). Broke glass pan for Ferns whilst washing it in water tank. Shifted plants of Pteris tremula into large pots to grow on for cutting, standing them in late Peach house. Gave catalogues which I did not want to W^m. Claydon.

Friday 3

Wind S.W. very strong all day and very drying, sky overcast at times during the day. Filled earthenware box with plants. Potted up into 60s & 48s Lobelias speciosa, pumila & a double one. Melons now throwing out fruit laterals, stopped some of them one joint beyond the fruit. Cinder ashes removed from pit in front of late vinery & soil forked up. Peaches in late house just beginning to colour. Large tub for manure water for Chrysanthemums cleaned out & put in tank to steep.

Saturday 4

Wind S.W., blowing freely, weather very changeable all day, few light showers during the day. Syringed Orchard house in mor^ing, cleaned plants in houses etc. M^r. Bryan went out early to Cambridge viz. 5.30 a.m. returned 3 p.m. Had M^r. Webster's horse & cart latter went to Lancashire with his daughter. Basket of plants came by carrier, Heathers & Azaleas from Cambridge M^r. Barnes I think. D^wf. Kidney beans sown in pit in front of late Vinery. Strawberries gathered by M^r. & M^rs. B. for preserving.

Sunday 5

Wind S. very bright 1st in morning; fine all day though slightly overcast at times. Self on duty. Had New Potatoes yesterday & today 1st this season, also green Peas.

Monday 6

Wind S. bright mor, dull middle of day, fine evening. Took out from vineries Azaleas which had finished their groth etc. and put in cooler houses to harden off, previous to going out of doors. Watered Cucumbers in frames with manure water, afterwards with clean water to cleanse them.

Tuesday 7   Wind S. fine day, dull midday, very hot when sun was out; clouds indicative of thunder. Camellias put outside under wall. Top-dressed 2 plts of Alocasia Metallica in Stove with rough fibrous peat & loam & silver sand roots of which had worked to surface. Rooted Strawberry runners in pots separated from old plants, variety Black Prince. Mr. Bryan out in evening with cart. James met him at Walden, brought horse back.

Wednesday 8   Wind S. fine day, warm. Shifted 2nd batch of Fuchsias into 48 size pots, gave some away to men. Hortal & Agrial Show at Bishop Stortford 1st day Mr. Bryan went. Self went to Walden in evening. Saw G. Webb, looked over Mr. Chater's Nursery, which was very gay with bedding plants etc. Measured for new pair of everyday boots, at Jeffrey's.

Thursday 9   Wind S. very bright mor, very hot all day, sun slightly veiled with a yellowish mist middle part of day. Went to Bishops Stortford in mor. by 10.23 train returned by mail at 10.20 pm, large number of people at all stns to B.S. Lost key of watch, not able to wind it up at night. Looked through houses of Mr. Ward Gr to Mr. Miller, some very fine grapes in

some of them. Vines growing freely at top and bottom, the former to cause sap to flow all over the plant, & latter to encourage production of new roots. Shoots at bottom allowed to ramble over border none being tyed to rafters except for new canes. Went to H. & A. Show, met there R. Adneth & H. Westley. Some fine specimen plants exhibited by Messrs. Ward Wheeler & Pineapple comp[ny], former taking lead in all classes who had huge plts of Bougainvillea glabra, Genytilles tulipera, Stephanotis, Phenocoma, Statico profusa, Arthurium sherzerianum & others.

Roses were poor, M[r.] Farren of Cambridge being foremost.

Saw jumping of horses at 4 p.m. in Agricul[al] till 6.30. Ponies done best. Helped H. Westley to pack up etc at night, came with him by rail as far as A. End.

Chrysanthemums set out at full distance in lower slip. Bouvardias planted out.

Friday 10	Wind S. fine day, very hot all day, became cloudy at 6 p.m. and Thunder commenced, rain falling at 7 p.m. falling gently all the evening, lightning (sheet) very sharp and very frequent. Potted off & shifted Begonias in Stove. Shifted Palms in Green house, also Capsicums into 24s, just showing flower buds, put in cool pit. Put in 1st lot of cuttings of Poinsettia pulcherima in Stove. Had new Key for Watch from Walden, wound up this morning with M[r.] Bryan's.
Saturday 11	Wind N. dull day, sun only shining faintly once or twice during the day, very close and warm, Thunder heard at 5 p.m. till 8, rain fell heavily during that time commencing at 7 p.m. Richardia Ethiopica shifted into larger pots, & put in pit. Picked out some of early Achimenes in Stove (in bloom), staked them and put them in pit. Cleaning up houses &c. Took out hardwooded plts done blooming and put in pit to make new growth. James stung by Bee on hand. Went to S. Walden late in evening, brought home Watch for James.
Sunday 12	Wind N.W. dull morning, bright & hot in after[n]. Stayed in all mor[ing]. Went to Walden church in after[n]. Went to M[r.] G. Webb's to tea stayed till 11.15 p.m. Very close & warm at night.
Monday 13	Wind N.W. fine bright mor, cloudy at times during the day. Rooted runners of Black Prince Strawberry separated from old plants and stood on

ashes in slip. Put up netting, to catch forwardest fruit in late Peach House. Cuttings of Pinks put in under bell glasses on north side of Orchard house shaded from hot sun.

Tuesday 14   Wind S.W. very warm but nice breeze. Shifted 1st lot of Chinese Primula's into 48s. Fruit trees in lower slip dusted with tobacco powder for fly. Potted 2 young seedlings of Clianthus Dauphini. Put in cuttings of Poinsettia pulcherima, Torenia asiatica & Echeveria retusa sinensis. James went out for 1st time this season in search of Wasps' Nests. Gooseberries & Currants being covered with nets for protection from birds.

Wednesday 15   Wind S.W. fine day throughout, bright and very hot. Small Cinerarias dusted with Tobacco powder to kill fly. Shifted half batch of Salvia splendens into 16 size pots.

Thursday 16   Wind S.W. very hot. Shifted young seedlings Cineraria's into 48s putting them in 3 light box under wall in Melon ground. Took up wire basket filled with plants for Her Ladyship's room. Early Peas & broad Beans pulled up & ground cleared for Autumn Cauliflowers, Celery etc. Went to Walden in evening bought pair of carpit slippers at 2/6.

Friday 17   Wind S.E. very bright & hot. Went up to house after breakfast with plants for large stand etc. All the family except Lord Braybrook came home by midday train. Part of zonal Geraniums put out doors & bloom picked off to come on later. Autumn cauliflowers planted in ground where Peas have been grown, the ground having been cleared of weeds not dug, firmness of soil beneficial to them. Celery planted out in beds 6ft wide with same distance between soil thrown out to depth of 18 inches, manure put in and dug up with bottom soil and well watered. Plants put out in rows across the bed 15 inches apart with 6 from plant to plant in the row.

Saturday 18   Wind N.E. sky quite clear all day, very hot middle of the day, cold last night with heavy dew, thermometer down to 35°, 96° in day in sun. Went up to house 1st in morning to clean & water plants on stand, vases, baskets, etc. Houses all cleaned up by 3 p.m. Double White Primula's taken from pit & put in 2 light box under wall near bothy. Gave a good soaking of water to Melons. Had new piece of hose for syringing Orchard house. Had fire in Stove at night to warm flue to take off excessive damp, night being cold. Had new pair of heavy boots for every day at Jeffreys, Walden, gave for them 16/6 – also porcupine Pen-holder having lost white one.

Sunday 19

Wind N.E. Dull & Damp with very heavy fog first in morning, rather cool, clearing off about breakfast time gradually getting clearer & hotter & remained very hot the rest part of the day. Self on duty, great deal of watering to do in afternoon, shut up Vineries at 4 p.m. Syringed, etc. Birthday of James Bedgegood.

Monday 20

Wind S.E. bright morning exceedingly hot throughout the day, thermometer standing at 90° in the shade, middle part of day. Shook out & repotted Pelargoniums Gauntlet & Snowdrop, they having been cut down & growing again freely. Mr. Ward, noted Pine & Grape grower, Bishop Stortford, called in with a gardener from Mr. Robinsons, Wendon. Mr. Bryan not in the way, self showed them through houses etc. their time being limited. Mr. Bryan angry for not sending for him.

Earthenware fern case (new) filled in place of one of glass accidently broke by me on the 2nd. Strawberry runners in pots, var. Black Prince for planting out, separated from old plants, taken up & set close under wall of mess room till wanted to plant out. Plums and large Cherry (in pots) with fruit nearly ripe removed from Orchard house to Early Vinery. Melons, shoots thinned out, other with fruit stopped, fruit already set raised on pots.

Self troubled in mind with several things lately taken place in affairs connected with situation, had thought of giving notice to leave.

Tuesday 21

Wind S.W. blowing rather strong, weather changeable, several showers during the day but from very light clouds.

Took plants up to house in place of those gone off Pelargoniums, Zonals & Balsams 1st batch of latter just coming into bloom. Brought away hanging basket to be lined with moss. Shifted young vines into 24s struck this spring from eyes; var. Gros Colman.

Took up rooted Strawberry runners President & Reens Seedling; Old plants of latter pulled up (forced last year & planted out), ground cleaned, drills drawn, watered & planted with green Kail. Filled small hanging basket in evening. Annual Dinner & Fete of Foresters at Walden.

Wednesday 22

Wind W. mild, dull nearly all day. Showery in evening. Began putting in cuttings of Verbena's starting with whites viz. Boule de Neige, cuttings very good, put in 24s pots, stood in cold frame to be kept close & shaded from sun by day & plenty of air by night.

Thursday 23 Wind W. very warm, cloudy 1st in morning, had fire lit, clearing off at 8 a.m. bright & cloudy alternately throughout the day, heavy thunder-storm at 1 p.m. rained in torrents about $1/2$ an hour. Horticultural Show at Cambridge, Mr. Bryan went, took with him fruit, Peaches & Grapes. Finished putting in Verbena cuttings of Pink & Purple (1st batch). Cut basket of Flowers & sent to Revd. Wicks of Littlebury by 4 p.m. Mr. Bryan obtained 1st prize each for Peaches, Nectarines & Grapes at Hortal Show at Cambridge.

Friday 24 Wind N.E. very clear & bright morning, cloudy about $1/2$ past 12 o'clock, Thunder storm commenced at 1 p.m. lasting nearly 2 hours, nice rain same time. Thunder was very heavy.
Shifted 2nd batch of Balsams ex 60s into 32s & 48s. Shook out & repotted Cyclamens (old plants) plunged full sun in ashes (in evening).

Took out Azaleas & other plants from 3rd Vinery to lessen supply of moisture. Grapes nearly ripe. Strawberries near Bees pulled up & thrown away; var. Black Prince layed in pots last year & planted out bore excellent crop this year.

Saturday 25   Wind N.W. cold 1st in morning, dull & cloudy with very heavy fog, cleared up towards midday, fine afternoon & evening. Houses all cleaned up, washed down etc. Went out in evening with Moule & James to destroy Wasps' nests; destroyed twelve by pouring in the hole a quantity of Tar.

Sunday 26   Wind S.W. dull & showery till 1.30 p.m. Fires lit in houses. Very fine A. & E. Went to Wendon church in A. & to Abbey Lane Chapel (Walden) in E. Liked service very much at both places.

Monday 27   Wind S.W. dull & showery nearly all day. Sun only shining little in afternoon. Netted Nectarines in late house to catch fruit. Put in more cuttings of Poinsettia pulcherima. Runners of Reens Seedling Strawberry (layed in 32 size pots) got up & stood on bed of ashes in slip. Fires lit in late Vinerys and Stove at night to dispell dampness. Began thinning Grapes in Orchard house in evening.

Tuesday 28   Wind S. very changeable, began raining at 7 a.m. fast till 10 a.m., showery all morning, fine in afternoon, but not much sun. Shifted part of last batch of Chrysanthemums into 16s, removed all to bottom slip. Strawberries (Black Prince) planted on border at end of early Vinery (this year's runners layed in (small) 60 size pots. Celery earthed up 1st time). Made 1 hour in morning thinning grapes in Orchard house. New chains (brass) put on hanging baskets. Fetched down one from her Ladyship's room in evening & filled with fresh plants.

Wednesday 29   Wind S. dull & foggy 1st in morning, clearing off at 7 a.m. sun very hot, few light showers towards midday, fine A. & E. Took up plants to house Dracaena Cooperii for top of stand. D. Guilfoilii for centre of basket in her Ladyship's room etc. Tops of Echeveria metallica (young plants but getting long) took off and inserted. Shifted winter blooming Salvia's from 60s into 32s standing them outside as before. Chrysanthemums & Strawberries dusted over with soot. Pots made ready for latter by the men for shifting them into size 32s.

Thursday 30   Wind N.W. fine bright morning up till 12.30 when throughout the rest part of day was more or less cloudy. Shifted Tree Carnations into 48s standing them in open pit. Plunged Centaurea gymnocarpa in leaf mould, in open pit. Took part of Eucharis amazonica from Stove to front slab in 3rd Vinery, to rest them before blooming. Ground where Potatoes have

been dug up, cleaned & planted with coleworts. Went to Walden in evening. School treat at A.E. Men from Pampisford Hall called to see M[r.] Bryan, one being Head G. there. M[r.] B. lent books to James on Geometry & Flower Gardening, latter Hardy &c. by Thompson.

Friday 31

Wind W. in morning changing in evening to S. very bright in morning, heavy clouds appearing at midday, dull afternoon, like storms. Pit of 3 lights made up for Cucumbers. Began shifting Strawberries (for forcing) into 32s; var. Reens seedling. Treat given to men at M[r.] Lyles's, Chesterford. M[r.] B. gone. Last day of Boy, for keeping birds ex crops &c.

AUGUST 1874

Saturday 1

Wind S.W. raining fast in M. till 7.30 a.m. dull all day, sun came out for few minutes at dinner time. Took Adiantums from 2nd Vinery put some in pit, others in 3rd Vinery under stage. Took Clerodendron Balfourii from Stove to ripen wood. Soil prepared and put in potting shed for Geranium cuttings. Bought Hymn book for Abbey Lane chapel also Union Tune book, gave for former 1/4 latter 4/6. Cucumb[rs] P. out 1st 3 lights.

Sunday 2

Wind S.W. blowing rather freely not much sun till afternoon. Self on duty, slept till 1/2 past 6 a.m.

Monday 3

Wind S.W. fine bright morning, fine all day. James went to Short Grove (S[gr] Smiths) first thing in morning to fetch Borage. Grand Fête & Gala of Ancient Shepherds at Walden, all men & women went from garden, self went in evening. Held in meadow, public sports & amusements stage and rope performance etc. Band of Rifle Volunteers in attendance.

Tuesday 4

Wind W. changing in evening to N.W. dull and showery all day. Shifting Strawberries into 32s. Dinner party at house in evening.

Wednesday 5

Wind N.W. fine morning, clear and bright till breakfast time when it became overcast & continued so all day with showers. Potting Strawberries finished R[ns] Seedling Early Potatoes being took up and dried and stored away in Potatoe house var Early Dalmahoy.

Thursday 6   Wind N.W. blowing strong all day clear bright morning, fine day. Took up plants to house for the decoration of His Lordships study for Ball tonight & Dinner party. Red Quarrenden Apples gathered, Veitch's Autumn Giant Cauliflower coming into use several been cut.

Friday 7   Wind S.W. very warm throughout the day. Cloudy at times & like rain. Finished potting Strawberries for forcing, Varieties Black Prince, President, and Reen's Seedling. Cucumber pit lined with hot dung (Plants just put in) viz. a few days.

Saturday 8   Wind S.W. nice rain last night or early this morning, few showers during the day, not very much sun, and not very drying. Finished all watering by 5.30 p.m. Put netting to some of Peaches in pots in Orchard house to catch fruit. Ground on which Cauliflowers had been grown, manured & dug up for Winter Spinach. Went home by 7.36 p.m. train from Audley End arriving at Cambridge 8.10. Met E.A.C. in town. Took back book lent to me by Mrs Chater (Title, Stove & Greenhouse plants, B.S.W.) Seed sown of Lettuce for Winter & Spring use, Varieties, Winter Cos, Hardy Cos & Hammersmith.

Sunday 9   Wind S.W. rather dull, few very light showers. Self at Grantchester, spent day at Vicarage with E.A.C., F.P. & H.C. Went to church M. & E. Went for walk after Tea through fields etc. Corn all appeared ripe great deal cut and carried.

Monday 10   Wind W. blowing rather strong, very showery, Sun very hot when out, Few peals of Thunder heard in afternoon, raining fast at night (fine rain). Netted latest tree in late Peach house, to catch fruit. Pelargoniums cut down & laid on their sides to ripen wood etc. Seed of Mignonette sown in 48 & 32 size pots in Peat & loam, put in pits & kept shaded till up; Never seen such soil used before.

Tuesday 11   Wind W. very strong all day, cloudy greater part of the day few showers in evening between 6 & 7 o'clock. Rather cold nights just now, Thermometer last night went as low as 34°. Put in more cuttings of Verbena's. Mr. Bryan gone out for few days. Went as far as Cambridge by 12.19 a.m. train ex Audley End.

Wednesday 12   Wind S.W. clear bright mor, heavy clouds arising about 8 a.m. dull at intervals throughout the day; very drying. Put in Pelargonium cuttings &

put them in pit. Runners cut off from Strawberries, litter cleared from between the rows & otherwise cleaned. Ground on which Potatoes were grown prepared by manuring & digging for planting out Strawberry layers (or runners). Sent C. Express to Mrs. Kennedy. James sent home. Cuttings of Geraniums var. Victor Lemoine, Vyde Lyon & Salvia patens.

Thursday 13   Wind S.W. mild, dull and showery all day. Shifted Cineraria's into 24 & 32 size pots standing them in open pit, to be protected from heavy rains with canvas coverings. Fire at night, at Duxford consisting of 3 hay stacks. Engine & men ready if wanted, did not go, fire raging from 8. to 11.30 p.m.

Friday 14   Wind S.W. stormy, not much sun. Shifted Dbl. Whte Primula's (had been divided & potted previously in all peat & sand but not done very well). Shifted into 48 & 32 size pots in rough leaf mould and little loam, with plenty sand, & put in pit. Winter Spinach sown, on ground were spring cauliflowers were grown, having been well manured dug up and firmly trod. Watered Cucumbers with manure water, afterwards with clean water to cleanse foliage etc.

Saturday 15   Wind S.W. fine morning, dull latter part of day, no rain except light shower late in evening. Cleaned up houses etc as usual. Shifted into 32 size pots Clerodendron fallax splendens, from Lyles & Speed, Cambridge. Went to Walden in evening. Bought Bristol Tune Book at Mr. Hart's at 3/6.

Sunday 16   Wind S.W. dull all day, sun only partly shining a time or two during the day. Putting shading on Stove when wind took it right over with pole, latter breaking square of glass. Very little watering to do.

Monday 17   Wind N. 1st in morning changing in afternoon to W. beautiful clear morning, fine all day. Began putting in cuttings of Centaurea ragusina. Carnations being layered.

Tuesday 18   Wind N.W. very close, dull just a few minutes sun early in morning & at 5 p.m. rained very fine a little time at Midday. Fruit trees in Orchard house pruned, finished putting in cuttings of Centaurea ragusina compacta & put in cold frame fully exposed to sun with just enough protection with lights to keep off heavy rains. Took them off with heal, trimmed off lower leaves

& cut off all others except the young centre one's leaving portion of stalk, inserted singly in the smallest pots, in leaf mould & sand, had soil rather moist so as not to be obliged to water for a time except a slight sprinkle overhead during the day.

Very warm in evening and looking like storms; Thermometer 70° at 8 p.m.

Wednesday 19 Wind W. very close & warm, cloudy till about 11 a.m. then gradually clearing off and was very hot & bright all rest part of day. Thermometer went up to 80° in the shade. Took out from Stove, last batch of Achimenes in bloom, & put in pits; Shifted few not in bloom into 24s to come on later. Mr. Bryan putting in cuttings of Geranium Manglesii in 24 size pots, standing on ashes, full sun. Took from Stove Euphorbia jacquinflora & Epyphyllum truncatum and put in Vineries to ripen wood. Smoked Stove in evening. Took out Adiantums in bloom.

Thursday 20 Wind W. rather foggy 1st in morning. Sky clear, bright hot day. Shifted Euphorbia jacquinflora into large pots put in Stove till rooted. Shifted also Gesneria exoniensis & G refulgens, into 32s & 48s & put on shelf in stove. Cuttings put in of Bronze Geraniums & stood in pit. First Melon cut & put on front slab in late Vinery to finish ripening. Smoked Stove at night for Thrip. Seed sown in open ground of Stewarts, early cabbage for Winter & spring use.

Friday 21 Wind W. very warm, cloudy & looked like rain in mor, but cleared off after breakfast. Went by Excursion train to Yarmouth arriving at 11.30 a.m. returned 6.30 p.m. reached Audley End at 11.5 p.m. Met E.A.C. and other Friends at Shelford & parted from them at night there. Had very nice day at Yarmouth. Went on Sea twice, sea rough 2nd time, 7 in boat seasick, including Self. Saw John Hughes, who was staying there with his Master, also Mr. & H. Glasscock. Had very pleasant journey, plenty of room &c. Corn late, about Norwich.

Saturday 22 Wind N.E. fine bright & clear day. Sun very hot. Went through cleaning in houses as usual. Noticed that Poinsettia's and Euphorbia's had suffered from the effects of Fumigation in stove; viz. leaves dropped. Filled (in evening) small baskets for Her Ladyship's room & took up by 8 p.m.

Sunday 23   Wind N.E. Sun hot in middle part of day. Went in mor. to Walden Church and in Evening to Abbey Lane Chapel, stayed in all afternoon looking over letters, etc.

Monday 24   Wind N.E. foggy & cold 1st in Mor. Thermometer had been down during night or morng to 35°. Cleared off by 8 a.m.; very hot in middle of day. Put nets to catch fruit round trees in Orchard house. Practising cricket in evening for Match next Thursday on lawn. Lord B – k bowling part of time, ball once knocked into river by Mr. Holdham.

Tuesday 25   W. N.E. very close & warm, Thundered a little from 5.30 to 6.30 a.m. light shower of rain sky rather heavy all day. Netting put over ventilation in 2nd Vinery. Soil, left from potting Strawberries, got into Hothouse shed to come in for forcing Kidney Beans. H & F came over in afternoon, went back by 7.00 p.m. train from Audley End.

Wednesday 26   Wind S.W. very dull & cloudy till 8 a.m., clearing off then till 3 p.m. dull again all afternoon. Bougainvillea glabra & Stephanotis floribunda taken out from Stove & put in early vinery to ripen wood. Shifted young Dracaena's into 48 & 32 size pots. Last of Peaches in 2nd house gathered, trees pruned & well syringed. Ground raised with forks between lately planted greens, and well watered. Filled large hanging basket for Her Ladyship's room and took up at 8 p.m. Went out on lawn at 5.15 p.m. to practise cricket.

Thursday 27   Wind S.W. very mild, dull, scarcely any sun. Cricket Match played on lawn between House & Stables resulting in favour of latter by 2 runs and 1 wicket to fall. Self played with Stables, began 11.15 a.m. finished 6.40 p.m. had dinner at 1.30 p.m. Mr. Bryan out with horse and trap.

Friday 28   Wind S.W. fine morning, cloudy at times during the day. Zonal Geraniums that have been standing outside & blooms kept off, shifted into 48 & 32 size pots and put in pit. Early celery earthed up (2nd time). Pelargoniums that have been cut down, set up and sprinkled overhead.

Saturday 29   Wind S.W. mild, rather showery, Thunder storm passed over at 3 to 3.30 p.m. accompanied by heavy shower of hail. Took out all plants of Alocasia macroriza variegata from Stove & put in late Vinery to complete groth. Onions for spring use sown on open border, also in frame (and protected from Birds with Nets). Asiatic & Early Urfurt cauliflower for spring use with protection through Winter. Went to Walden in evening, bought black necktie, collars & cuffs, also writing paper.

Sunday 30

Wind S.W. very mild, fine bright morning, cloudy at times during the day, also in evening, rain at night. Annual sermons for schools preached at Walden, morning by the Bishop of Rochester & in evening by Bishop Clatton (Archdeacon of London). The latter preaching at Littlebury in afternoon. Both staying at Lord Braybrooks. Self on duty. Servants came down in morning to look over Garden.

Monday 31

Wind S.W. rather strong, fine, though cloudy at times but very drying up till 4 p.m. then became dull and rained (very fine) in evening. Putting netting to Fruit trees in Orchard house. Early Potatoes taken up & stored in P. house. Received from Mr Bryan £3-9-4 for Month's wages, also notice to leave at end of next month.

SEPTEMBER 1874

Tuesday 1

Wind S.W. rather high, dull & cloudy, scarcely any sun all day, few showers afternoon and evening. Shifted Begonia's into 48s & 32s in Stove, also Lycopods into same sizes. Potted of Torenia Asiatica (rooted cuttings). Put in cuttings of Iresine Lindenii. Hot lining put to late cucumbers.

Wednesday 2

Wind W. fine day, very drying. Removed Capsicums (fruit nearly full size flowers on also) from pit to Early Vinery to ripen fruit. Fuchsias that have bloomed once, been cut in & grown on again outdoors, just coming into bloom, put in pit in place of Capsicums. Shifted into larger pots Adiantum Farleyense & Sphaerogene latifolia in soil consisting of equal parts Peat & Loam, with sand. Began to stake Chrysanthemums, (specimens), Onions (White Spanish) pulled up and put together to dry. Went out in evening to destroy Wasp's Nest's, took 14, dug out one been destroyed few days, with hole 2 feet in diameter.

Thursday 3

Wind S.W. very close & warm, dull all day. Put in cuttings of Heliotrope. Staking Chrysanthemums in shed, being showery. Wind changed in evening, to North, rained very heavily.

Friday 4   Wind S.W. fine & bright 1st in morning coming over cloudy about 9 or 10 o'clock, showery rest part of day. Staking Chrysanthemums for Exhibition.

Saturday 5   Wind S.W. fine & bright early in morning, clouds appearing after breakfast, but not enough to hide the sun till afternoon when it was dull but no rain. Syringe Stove now at midday or about 10 a.m. rather than in afternoon, as it can be done more effectually without keeping so wet for the night, having more time to dry.

Ground (on which Veitch's cauliflower has been grown & cut) heavily manured, dug up & well trod to be planted with President Strawberry (young plants).

Sunday 6   Wind S.W. very dull all day, showery at Midday. Went to Littlebury church in afternoon, Walden in evening.

Monday 7   Wind S.W. dull all day, no rain till evening. Cricket Match (return) played on lawn, won by Stables in one inings with 273 runs. M^r. Hasley making 110. Self stumped out 1st ball by Webster. Had Dinner & Tea in servants hall. Wickets pitched at 11.0 a.m. drawn at 6.30 p.m.

Tuesday 8   Wind S.W. fine day though cloudy at times. Cleared out all plants from Stove & put in Vineries. Stove to be thoroughly cleaned, painted etc. Harvest Festival at Littlebury had hymns 335, 238, 223, 224, 136 H. A. & M. Grand Floral Fête at Sawbridgeworth. James & M^r. Bryan went.

Wednesday 9   Wind S.W. fine 1st in morning, coming over cloudy after breakfast, between that & dinner, rain fell in torrents few peals of Thunder, fine afternoon. Horticultural Show at Walden of Flowers & Fruit & Vegetables, no plants for competition. A Stand of 12 very fine Dahlias from M^r. Glasscock of Bishops Stortford. Went over with Moul in evening, very dull affair, no music, scarcely any Visitors. M^r. Barnes over from Cambridge. M^r. Bryan met him at station with horse & cart and drove him there again at night. Earliest Celery earthed up for last time.

Thursday 10   Wind S.W. fine & bright all the morning cloudy at times during the afternoon, Thunder storm passed over about 2.15 p.m. but no rain, very much like storms at night. Winter Spinach thinned out to single plants 2 or 3 inches apart.

Friday 11

Wind S.E. very dull all day, no sun at all showery, rough at night & raining very fast. Mr. Bryan went out with horse & cart at 12.30 p.m. returned at 10.0 p.m. Helped to take out horse etc. Potted off second sowing of Cineraria's. Put in cuttings of Alternanthera's and Golden Star-wort or Stellaria graminea aurea (New bedding plants). Lettuce seed sown in open ground vars Hammersmith, Winter Cos & Brown Cos.

Saturday 12

Wind W. dull but no rain, mild. Shifted young plants of Poinsettia pulcherima into 48s. Noticed that Centaurea cuttings (striking in 3 light box on ashes) were much fresher, stood up better & were better rooted where partly shaded from sun by sides of box, etc.

Sunday 13

Wind N.W. beautifully fine all day very warm in morning. Self on duty nothing much required water except Chrysanthemum's. Harvest Festival at Walden Church in evening. Sermon preached by Rev^d. Carter Vicar of Duxford.

Monday 14

Wind N.W. fine, rather drying. Bulbs came in from James Carter & Co. Potted Early Roman Hyacinths into small 60s large 60s & 48s singly & in 3s & 5s, and put in corner of shed & covered with sand.

Tuesday 15

Wind N. beautiful clear & fine morning and though clouds arose as the day got up it was very fine & dry all day. Took hard wooded plants from pits into greenhouse again, brought out from latter, Myrtles & other plants infested with Thrip & gave them a good syringing. Shifted Early fl Pelargoniums (Gauntlet & Snowdrop) spring struck cuttings, into 48s & put in pits. Potted into 48s Lachenalia tricolor 15 in a pot, the bulbs had some of them started growing, put them in pit close to the glass.

Wednesday 16

Wind S.W. very dull all day, few light showers early in the morning & also in the evening, very mild Thermometer standing at 60° Farht. Old plants of Pelargoniums that have been cut down & just breaking again got into pits under glass. Solanum hybridum (planted out on Peach border,) taken up & potted & stood out of doors under north wall till established. The berries on them set & nearly full size but they had flowers on also.

Thursday 17

Wind S.W. very dull & rather showery till 2.30 p.m. clearing up then and was a fine sunny afternoon. Primula's & Cineraria's got under cover in pits etc. Shifted spring-sown seedling Cyclamens into 48s & large 60s. Horticultural Show at Cambridge M^r. B gone with fruit etc.

Friday 18	Wind S.W. fine day, cloudy at times. Cyclamens that were potted & plunged out of doors with those potted yesterday, put into pit where Melons were grown, the top of the old soil having been taken off and a layer of cinder ashes put on with an outer lining of hot dung, the latter having also been put to cucumbers in same range. Onions pulled up on 2nd now cleaned, got in and stored in loft.
Saturday 19	Wind S.W. fine day, very warm, rather dull in afternoon, cloud indicative of rain, mild at night, Thermometer 58°. Dusted Verbena's over with Tobacco powder to destroy Thrip & other insects, cuttings put in of Scented geraniums.
Sunday 20	Wind S.E. fine day though not very bright rather dull 1st in morn few light showers in evening at from 7.30 to 9.0 p.m. Went to Walden church M. & E. and to Wenden in A. Harvest sermon preached at latter. Banns of Marriage publish^d at Littlebury church between G. Dasley & Selina Whitehead for 1st time.
Monday 21	Wind S.E. Beautiful fine morning, very mild shower of rain at 4.30 p.m. Threw away useless plants in Green-house & took in few large Azalea's and all Camellia's from outside. Ground on which Onions were grown cleaned by howing & raking (not dug) and planted with Cabbages. Mr. Bryan gone to London. Gardener from Revd. Latimer Neville's called, gave him cutting's of Verbena's & other things. Made up bouquet for Mrs. Brown (one of Garden women).
Tuesday 22	Wind S.E. rather strong, beautiful bright & clear mor, fine day rather cloudy in afternoon. Shifted Kennedys Monophylla into 16 size pot &

trained on baloon trellis. M^r. Bryan came home from London by first train. M^r. Woodman, G^r at Babraham hall with 2 others called at 10.0 a.m. stayed till 5.0 p.m. tyed up for them cuttings of Alosia citriodona and Fuchsia Sunray.

Wednesday 23 Wind S.E. very dull all day, rain fell heavily from 10.0 a.m. till 12.30. Potatoes pitted & covered over with Straw soil etc sorts were Dalmahoy & Suttons Red skinned Flourball. Mixed up soil for potting Hyacinths and other bulbs. Sent letter to Veitchs with form (filled up), also recommendation from M^r. B.

Thursday 24 Wind S.W. fine day, mild. Potting Bulbs, viz. Hyacinths, Narcissus set out of doors under north wall to be covered over with cinder ashes. Wm Claydon stayed in evening & had Tea & Supper with us, leaving about 11.0 p.m. Beautiful fine night, Moon shining very brightly.

Friday 25 Wind W. very fine and bright day sky clear, except from 1.0 to 3.0 p.m. Sun very hot. Applied shading in Middle part of day to cucumbers, Primulas, Cinerarias & other things. Potted Tulips, which completed potting of bulbs. Put Netting to last of Peaches in Orchard house.

Saturday 26 Wind W. rather foggy in morning, fine day, very bright & hot Thermometer over 70° in shade. Cleaned up houses etc Brought in Azalea's & put in Green house.

Sunday 27 Wind S.W. very fine day, not over bright but very close & warm. Self on duty.

Monday 28 Wind S.W. fine day, very warm, cloudy at times. Began getting plants in Stove again, cleaning them, etc. William Claydon left Littlebury to go to M^r. Speeds Gonville Nursery, Cambridge. Self went to Walden in evening. Posted to M^r. Unwin, cuttings of Fuchsia Sunray. Called to see M^r. Webb at 9.0 p.m. stayed till 12.0 p.m.

Tuesday 29 Wind S.W. rather strong, sunny greater part of day but not very bright, shower of rain at 4.30 p.m. clouds indicative of storms towards evening. Arranging plants in Stove. Caladiums (dried off) stored away under stage in Stove. Peach trees in Early house all stripped of their leaves being for most part quite green. Packed up all things in box ready to go away.

Wednesday 30 Wind S.W. fine day. Finished arranging plants in Stove took in Adiantiums Epyphyllum's & Euphorbia's (jacquiniflora). Went to Walden in afternoon, looked over M^r. Chaters Nursery with M^r. G. Webb. Left the service of Lord Braybrook, left Audley End for Cambridge by 7.35 p.m. train.

OCTOBER 1874

Thursday 1 Wind S.W. Weather very changeable very showery in afternoon. Unpacked box in Morning. Went to Cambridge in afternoon with E. A. C. to home. Had to take shelter from rain at Newnham Croft, too wet to return at night.

Friday 2 Wind S.W. rather strong, very wet 1st in morning till 11 or 12 oclock came home ex C. with E. A. C. arrived in at G– 9.30 a.m. fine in afternoon. At V– in evening.

Saturday 3 Wind S.W. blowing very strong. All day at home in morning reading etc. Went to Cambridge in afternoon. Calm starlight night. Gunpowder explosion at Regents Canal, 3 men killed, great deal of damage done to surrounding buildings, occurred at 5.0 a.m. before people were astir or it might have been worse.

Sunday 4 Wind S.W. rather cold, fine day beautiful clear night. Went to G. church Mor & Evening. Sermon in M. by Rev^d. Marcus ex London, in E. by Rev^d. Wm Martin, had tune Salem in Mor.

M.A.A. came in afternoon, stayed for E. service. Rode home with Rev^d. Marcus to Cambridge in carriage with Alfred.

Monday 5 Wind W. cold 1st in Morning, beautiful fine day. Cleared up flower garden in front of house at home (in M). Went in afternoon to V– E.A.C. being alone. Went to meet E.G. in E. ex Camb^ge. Mother had Grapes from Professor Clark's for making wine 6lbs at 4d per lb, (black) asked by H.C. to represent him at Wedding of G. Dasley & Selina Whitehead at Littlebury on 10th (assented).

Tuesday 6 Wind S. very strong, mild, cloudy & very much like storms, few light showers in afternoon and evening. Stayed indoors in Mor putting up shelves for Plants in kitchen window. Went in afternoon to Cambridge with E.A.C. Met M.A.A. at Newnham, went shopping etc, had Necktie ex E.A.C.

Mrs. Carltons 52nd birthday had some very good presents stayed to tea, arrived at G. at night 9.15 p.m.

Wednesday 7 Wind W. dull cloudy morning rained in torrents from 11.0 till 12.30 in morning, fine in afternoon. Wrote out Tunes in Bristol Tune Book. Spent evening with Mr Lowe. Mrs. Cutting called, stayed to tea.

Thursday 8 Wind W. beautiful clear & fine day. Went in morning to Gnd Mother U Johns etc Sale of Nursery stock, fruit trees, Roses & other things by Mr. Cutting called in on way from C–ge, very few buyers, Mr. Bester bought in great many things.

Friday 9 Wind S. looked rather stormy in morning, very heavy rain about 12 o'clock, fine afternoon and evening. Went to Mrs. Carltons to put in box edging prune Gooseberries etc. Came home with George.

Saturday 10 Wind S.W. very mild, beautiful fine & clear day. Marriage of Geo Dasley & Selina Whitehead at Littlebury by Revd Cooke, Curate of Walden. Went ex Cam in Mor by 9.45 a.m. train returning ex Chesterford 5.57 p.m. Spent evening at their lodgings at 24 Russell St. ages of both, 34 yrs.

Sunday 11 Wind S. very mild, clouds indicative of storms, light shower at 10 a.m. fine evening. Went to G church in Mor with E.A.C. & in afternoon to Cambridge. Stood as God-Father for Mrs. Buttresses daughter, baptized at Christ Church. Came home in carriage with Mr. Unwin. Wedding of S. Brown & S. Hett took place at Trumpington at 8.0 a.m.

Monday 12 Wind S.W. beautiful clear fine day & very mild. Helping Father to do up graves in new burial ground. Went to Cambridge in afternoon to Mr. Bashams about work etc looked over garden with Jacobs. Bought jacket & trousers for every day, came home with H.C. & G.

Tuesday 13 Wind S.W. mild, fine day. At home in mor. writing letters to U. Bromley, Mr. Webb and to Publisher of G. Chronicle with an advertisement for insertion in that journal for situation as U. gardener. Sent with it 2/6 in stamps. Went to Cambridge in afternoon to post them, E.A.C. going same time, so went together.

Wednesday 14 Wind S.W. close & warm, dull all day. Went over to Long Stowe Hall to see Mr. & Mrs. Claydon, with E.A.C. Caught 12.51 train from Lords Bridge Stn returning at night ex Old North Road 7.40 going on to Cambridge, rather showery after arriving at Stowe, heavy rain in afternoon about 3.30. 5 other Gentlemen went same time among whom were Mr. Deiper, Mr. Marshall, Wheat Sheaf & Mr Scott, Queens College. Saw nice plants in full bloom of Bougainvilleas glabra, had some talk with Mr. Claydon about going to work with him, made no agreement.

Thursday 15 Wind S.W. mild, very showery all day. Went to Cambridge in morning, looked over Nursery of Messrs Lyles & Speed agreed with Mrs. Chater to work for a week at the mill road garden getting things ready for sale etc. Reached home 6.30 M.A.A. came over in afternoon, wet night, went home with her to C. reached G. again 11.30.

Friday 16 Wind S.W. very wet dull dreary day. At home with "cold", sore throat etc layed in bed till 11.30 a.m. E.A.C. came in afternoon, went back & spent the evening with her, E.G. being out at Riversdale.

Saturday 17 Wind S.W. fine mor till 10 or 10 o'clock, very showery rest part of day. Went to Mrs. Carltons, dug up border etc.

Sunday 18 Wind W. fine day. Went to Grantchester church M. A. & E. Revd H home again.

Monday 19 Wind S.W. very much like storms 1st in morning few heavy showers before breakfast beautifully fine rest part of day. Went to work for Mrs. Chater at Mill Road Garden, painting Greenhouse, etc.

Tuesday 20 Wind S.W. beautiful fine day, warm. At work at Mill Road painting etc.

Wednesday 21 Wind S.W. very high & strong, stormy. Sale by Auction at Mill Road garden of Nursery stock etc, things made fair price. Went in evening to Harvest Festival at St Andrews the Great with E.A.C. & M.A.A. service over at 9.30 p.m. Hallelujah chorus sung at close of service. Sermon by Revd Carter.

Thursday 22 Wind W. very fine day. Working at Mill Road till 2.30. Came home to Tea party in behalf of Reading room, singing & reading in evening. Bought new felt hat at Cambridge at 5/-. M^rs. Hall (Jane Papworth) delivered of a Son at New Castle on Tyne.

Friday 23   Wind N.W. slight frost in morning, beautiful fine day but rather cold. Painting fence etc at Mill road.

Saturday 24   Wind W. very mild, dull all day. Working at Mill road garden painting gates. Went in evening into the Town, getting home 8.0 p.m. M^r. Rowe "Silversmith Market Hill" died at 4.0 p.m. from effects of Paralatic stroke very recently.

Sunday 25   Wind S.W. very mild, cloudy all day and very indicative of storms, heavy damp falling at times during the day, rained fast at night. Went to Grantchester church Morning and Afternoon, spent Evening at V– with E.A.C. M^rs. Martin in doors all day having bad cold.

Monday 26   Wind S.W. mild, wet showery morning, fine latter part of day. At home in morning writing name etc in books. Went in afternoon to Cambridge in search of employment. Called at Nurseries of Lyles & Speed, Willers, also Botanic garden.

Tuesday 27   Wind S.W. very close & warm, rather dull. Went to Mill Road garden, finished painting, cut remainder of grapes, & other work. Spent part of evening at Free Library. Came home with H. & G. Overtook E. Gladwell at Newnham.
                Father at night work for M^rs. N–d's removing night soil from W.C. with Wm Stearn.

Wednesday 28 Wind S.W. very mild, rather dull in morning, beautifully fine afternoon. At home all day, wrote letters to office's of Gardeners Chronicle and "Garden" with 5/- in stamps for 4 insertions of advert for situation in latter, former for enquiries as to cost of 4, ditto. Wrote also to J.R.S. 10 Perry Mill sending view of Audley End. Thinned Turnips in garden in afternoon. Spent evening at V–.

Thursday 29   Wind S.W. mild, very dull in morning, clearing up towards midday, fine in afternoon & very warm, heavy clouds rising towards evening, few peals of Thunder about 5 p.m. with light shower of rain. Went to Cambridge

Botanic Garden, saw M^r. Mudd (curator) about situation, requested to call on Monday next. Funeral of M^r. Roe, Market Hill took place.

Friday 30	Wind N. somewhat colder than yesterday, very dull all day, showery in morning. Went to Cambridge in evening, bought trousers in Sussex St for every day use at 9/-. Had hair cut at Hagger's Peas Hill. M^rs. Chater having front of shop, shutters etc painted. Came home with G. Tabor, reached home 6.45. E.A.C. came out for an hour in evening, went for walk to Trumpington, called in to see M^r. Lowe, went over Mill, was weighed by M^r. Lowe myself 10st 6lbs. E.A.C. 9st 10lbs. Fine starlight night.
Saturday 31	Wind N. dull very showery in morning. Went to Cambridge in afternoon, finished cleaning up Mrs. Carltons garden, planted Gooseberries for M^rs. Buttress, latter suffering from cold and Face ache, having had a tooth taken out. M.A.A. unwell.

NOVEMBER 1874

Sunday 1	Wind N.E. rather cold, very dull all day, no rain. Went to St Marks church in morning with H.C., sat with choir. good congregation. Afternoon and evening at Granchester. Beautiful sermon in aft by Revd Howard from Rev 7- part of 12 ver. Sermon in Even^g by Rev^d M^r. Chas Loxley 5th chap Matthew 8th ver. M^rs. Carlton & M.A.A. came over, had tea at V. stayed to E. service. Self went home with them as far as Newnham. E.A.C. has Rheumatics in neck & left shoulder.
Monday 2	Wind N.E. very dull in morning and rather showery, cleared off and was fine in afternoon. Went in morning to Botanic Garden, engaged with M^r. Mudd to work in the garden at 16/- per week with lodgings, to start on the 9th. Lizzie went to Revd Howard's as Nurse to children of Mrs. F. Howard, who arrived today from Switzerland. Self spent evening at V.– E.A.C.s neck better.
Tuesday 3	Wind S.E. very foggy 1st in morning, clearing off by 8.0 a.m. beautiful clear, bright, sunny day. At home in morning clearing Turnips, in garden, from weeds, & thining them out, late sowing of Veitch's Autumn Giant Cauliflower now coming into use. Went in afternoon with E.A.C. to

Cambridge. Had tea with M^rs. Apthorpe. Called to see F.P. at Avenue. Came home via Trumpington. Beautiful fine night, reached G. 9.0 p.m.

Wednesday 4 Wind S.E. foggy morning, fine clear day. At home all day, nailed up White Jasamine on house. Dug up piece of ground and put out Cabbage plants trod well the ground before planting. Spent evening at the Reading Room. Mother went with Lizzie to the Hospital; Examined by the House Doctor, Name of Dr Latham given on her paper, received some powders & requested to go again on the 14th.

Thursday 5 & Wind S.E. foggy nights & mornings with beautiful fine days. Digging up
Friday 6 ground on which Potatoes were grown after giving it a good coat of manure. Fire on 6th at Rose Crescent at the shop of Mr Farren Photographer at 1.0 a.m.

MAY 1875

Tuesday 11 Beautiful fine day, very warm. Quarrel between M^r. M. & family blows struck by him, about 5.0 p.m.

Wednesday 12 Fine day. Planted out Dahlia's on herbaceous ground, (old plants which had been started in-doors & cuttings taken from them.) Went home in afternoon to Bazaar or Garden party towards the funds for enlarging the church, a great many people present.

Monday 17 Began to put out bedding plants at Botanic Garden. Weather has been very warm. Plants all well hardened off.

Saturday 22 Wind S.W. rather strong, has been very showery since Tuesday. Greater part of bedding plants now out, putting out plants to-day round the houses on border.

DECEMBER 21st 1875

Henry Wainwright hung at Newgate at 8 a.m. for the murder of Harriet Louisa Lane, at 215 Whitechapel London (no confession).

Commentary

The following are notes to help the reader of William Cresswell's diary identify the people and places mentioned, as well as descriptions of the gardening techniques he is using. Words in **bold** indicate a separate entry.

GARDENING TECHNIQUES AND PRACTICES

Bees, swarms of: Swarms belong to the first person who hives the bees regardless of where they originally come from. It used to be thought that Sunday was the most likely day to catch a swarm as they could be unsettled by the sound of church bells. Noise could also make them settle and legends dating back to the Roman period claim that 'tanging' brass or iron objects together was the best method. Various other ways of taking a swarm include smoking, but the key is to capture the queen and the rest of the swarm will follow. A swarm would be taken in a straw 'skep'. A well-known country verse states:

A swarm of bees in May is worth a load of hay;
A swarm of bees in June is worth a silver spoon;
A swarm of bees in July is not worth a fly.

Bell glasses: Decorative and effective protection for plants often in the shape of a glass bell.

Bothy: Accommodation for unmarried under-gardeners. At **Audley End** House the Bothy was built in the 1820s at the back of the **Vinery** range so the gardeners were living close to both the boilers and the glasshouses and could therefore monitor heating and ventilation more effectively. There were three rooms in the Bothy comprising kitchen/living room and two bedrooms. This was where William Cresswell lived in 1874 and it is now displayed as it would have looked in his time – complete with a facsimile of his diary.

Box edging: Low clipped hedges of box (*Buxus sempervirens*) used for edging paths, borders and beds. The dense roots of the plants form an excellent barrier which prevents soil from spilling out onto the paths or lawns.

Cleaning plants: Routine general maintenance – removing dead leaves; checking for pests and diseases; picking over spent flowers to increase flowering; weeding; removing moss or liverwort etc. This has always been the best practice for plant hygiene.

Coal ashes: Used to stand pots on for drainage. The sharpness of the ashes also deterred slugs and snails.

Engine: Water tank on wheels with a syringe – ideal for spraying/watering.

Furnaces: Boilers lit to keep vineries/glasshouses to a required temperature.

Guano: Bird droppings used as fertiliser. Chicken manure was often used, and canary guano also seems to have been available at this time (*see* photograph page 133). Some was imported from South America on the return voyage of merchant ships.

Handlights/lights: Glazed panels, also known as 'dutch' lights, that sit on top of cold-frames or are used like cloches and propped up to protect plants in situ. It is normally a morning job for the gardener to assess the weather and then adjust the glazed protection as necessary. In the Victorian period lights varied in shape and design; some were made of glass encased in wood while others were made of leaded lights.

THE HYDRONETTE.

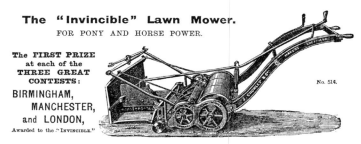

The "Invincible" Lawn Mower.

FOR PONY AND HORSE POWER.

The FIRST PRIZE
at each of the
THREE GREAT
CONTESTS:
BIRMINGHAM,
MANCHESTER,
and LONDON,
Awarded to the "INVINCIBLE."

No. 514.

Above, left: An advertisement in a Victorian catalogue for a watering device; right: In the late 19th century lawnmowers were often pulled by horses or ponies and the account books at Audley End reveal that special boots were purchased for the horses to wear to protect the grass **Opposite:** *A Victorian straw beehive on display at the Museum of Garden History in London; page 110: The Pond Garden viewed from the walled Kitchen Garden*

Horticultural Show: William Cresswell records exhibiting at shows in Cambridge, **Saffron Walden** and Bishops Stortford. These were events where gardeners could show off their skills as well as advertise the prowess of their staff. Gardeners around the country would meet up and discuss all the latest developments in horticulture, and the shows were an important part of the network by which knowledge was spread. No doubt the head gardeners also discussed their staff and passed them on to each other.

India rubber pipe: This may well have come from the India Rubber Works in Streatham run by P B Cow. The company was based in a former Georgian silk mill in Factory Square, opposite the south-west corner of Streatham Common. During the Second World War the company made 'Mae Wests' and later in the 20th century produced their famous 'Li-Lo' beds. In 1986 the factory was acquired by Sainsbury's who built a large supermarket on the site.

Lawn mowing: The first lawnmower had been built in 1830 and early machines were large and heavy needing two men or a horse to use them. By the 1870s a range of lighter, more efficient lawnmowers were available.

Lime and sulphur: Used as a fungicide.

Liquid manure: A simple fertiliser. In a letter of 12 March 1874 **Lady Braybrooke** complains that: 'When ever the roses have to be watered it is always done with something bought at Carters altho. growers of good roses say liquid manure from the stable yard is the best.'

However, some 'recipes' for liquid manure appear quite complicated. A 19th-century gardener's book in the collection of the Museum of Garden History, London, advocates mixing 2 pecks of sheep or deer dung, 1 peck of soot and 2 quarts of potter's guano into a smooth paste with boiling water and adding to a hogshead of rain water. The mixture had to be frequently stirred for a day or two and then a quart of quick lime added. It was ready for use when the liquid had become clear and had to be applied diluted with about 1/3 of clear water to plants in vigorous growth or in bloom.

Netting fruit: Individual nets put round each fruit to prevent it falling on the floor and bruising. This practice is still continued today.

Orchard House: A glasshouse built in the Kitchen Garden at **Audley End** in 1856 to the designs of Thomas Rivers, the great Victorian nurseryman who ran an extensive business in Sawbridgeworth, Hertfordshire. He invented and promoted these structures which were designed for the intensive production of dwarf fruit trees grown in pots on raised beds. At the end of each season the roots were pruned back so that the trees could remain in the same pot for many years. The Orchard House at Audley End is a particularly fine example. William Cresswell's diary reveals that he also used the Orchard House for other purposes, such as potting off geraniums.

Peach house: Peaches and nectarines were almost as popular as grapes during the Victorian period. The early and late peach houses at **Audley End** had a variety of fan-trained trees growing against the walls so the risk of frost spoiling the fruit crop was avoided.

Pits: Glass-topped growing frames partially sunk into the ground, like those at Heligan, Cornwall. The sides are perforated with vents and rotting manure is heaped up against the sides. As the manure rots, the organic processes give out heat which in turn heats the growing frame to a relatively constant temperature. The manure is turned to add oxygen to prolong the composting process. When the manure is past its best for heating, it is then ideal for adding to the soil elsewhere in the garden. Manure is a very environmentally sound source of energy, but rather labour intensive.

Plunging: Probably refers to a short-term display, or nursery bed, made up with plants still in their original clay pots. It looked just like a planted-out bed and had the added advantage that the clay pots would not dry out so quickly. The pots were sunk just below the surface of the soil or sand and could be changed regularly. As labour was cheap at this time, the wealthy could even afford to have beds changed for one-off special events.

Pot sizes: William Cresswell makes reference to a variety of sizes. The number of pots that could be made from a standard lump of clay determined the size of the pot. The most likely equivalent is as follows:

Pot sizes by 'cast'* of clay	Diameter at top	Depth
16s	9$^1/_2$ ins (24.1 cm)	9 ins (22.9 cm)
24s	8$^1/_2$ ins (21.6 cm)	8 ins (20.3 cm)
32s	6 ins (15.2 cm)	6 ins (15.2 cm)
48s	4$^1/_2$ ins (11.4 cm)	5 ins (12.7 cm)
60s	3 ins (7.6 cm)	3$^1/_2$ ins (8.9 cm)

*The 'cast' of clay was a predetermined volume

Pruning and nailing: Pruning the fruit trees growing against the garden walls; these would be espaliers and fan-trained specimens. Unwanted shoots and branches needed cutting back to keep the tree in shape and to ensure abundant harvests. Nails were put into the mortar so that branches could be tied into position. The mortar in the brick walls of the Kitchen Garden at **Audley End** is pitted from generations of gardeners training trees.

Short dung: As 'short' is another word for 'crumbly' this probably refers to dung fine enough to mulch. Bulky, unrotted manure is unsuitable for this job and, as it heats up considerably while it is breaking down, it cannot be put round tender plants. William would have used the unrotted manure in the **pits**.

Smoked the house: This would have been done with **Tobacco**.

Soot: Soot was used as an insecticide and a fungicide. As it is slightly caustic, it is not a nice substance to use all the time. Soot is added to the soil to increase the speed at which it can warm up, as well as for slug/snail 'rings' around the base of plants prone to damage.

Stove: A hothouse glasshouse where plants and flowers needing the highest temperatures were kept.

Strawberries: A popular glasshouse crop often placed on a high shelf in the **Vinery** range to ripen quickly.

Tan: Waste from the tanning process. Tannin is extracted from the bark of trees, particularly oak, larch and willow, in order to tan leather. The refuse makes ideal hotbeds as it provides a steady heat which can be maintained and regulated for a far longer period than stable manure.

Tobacco: A very effective horticultural fumigant still in use today. Now it is in the form of a cone-shaped candle, rather than paper, and is only used in private or commercial glasshouses because of the long airing period required before anyone can re-enter. The practice is to light the tobacco at the far end of the glasshouse and then work towards the door for obvious reasons! Deaths from incorrect use still occur – it is said to be like the poisoning effect of thousands of cigarettes in just a few breaths. Tobacco was also used as an insecticide – a 19th-century gardener's book advises immersing geraniums in a mixture of ¼ lb tobacco, 1 lb soft soap and 5 gallons of water to kill greenfly. Liquid made from tobacco is no longer recommended as an insecticide.

William Cresswell's pocket watch which he used throughout his life.

Vine border: Area under the grape vines where other plants could be grown.

Vinery: Glasshouse mainly used for growing grapes for the table. By the Victorian era the pineapple had been replaced by the grape as the most popular hothouse plant and well-to-do households expected a supply of fresh grapes throughout the year. Extensive vineries were built with sloping roofs and long lengths of rafters so the vines could be trained close to the glass to ripen the fruit as efficiently as possible. There were early and late vineries where the gardeners had to continually monitor the health of the vines, fumigating, spraying and adjusting heating and ventilation levels as necessary. Skilful pruning, training, feeding and watering were also required to ensure a succession of perfect fruit. A gardener who worked in the vineries had to have a high level of horticultural expertise.

The Vinery range at **Audley End** is one of the largest and earliest surviving examples in the country. It was built in the 1820s and has five separate bays giving a variety of growing conditions for different plants. At the back of the vineries, the shaded north side of the wall, is a long range of service buildings including the **Bothy**.

Weather report: William Cresswell makes a detailed weather report every day. This was usual practice, especially for a young gardener, and still forms part of the training of professional gardeners and horticulturalists today. Weather records are extremely useful for comparing plant growth and production figures from year to year. Checking through the records reminds the gardener what seasonal tasks need doing, and the season and weather also dictates what can feasibly be done. Having a record of weather conditions demonstrates to an employer what tasks could and couldn't be accomplished and why.

Winding up watches: It was important that the under-gardeners synchronised their watches with the Head Gardener.

PLACES

A.E.: Audley End. Situated on the edge of the town of **Saffron Walden** in Essex, this extraordinary mansion and its spectacular gardens have had a long history and varied fortunes – sometimes being more sumptuous than the royal palaces and at others teetering on the brink of demolition.

The estate stands on ground where the Benedictine priory of Walden was founded in 1140. The monastic foundation soon became immensely wealthy and powerful but was suppressed by Henry VIII during the dissolution of the monasteries in the 16th century and given to Sir Thomas Audley, Lord Chancellor of England. He knocked down much of the church but incorporated some of the abbey buildings into the new house he erected on the site. The name Audley End dates from around this time and is derived from Sir Thomas Audley's ownership and the estate's position at the extremity of the parish of Saffron Walden.

Audley's grandson, Thomas Howard, inherited the property in 1582, and was created Earl of Suffolk and Lord Chamberlain of the Household by James I. Howard needed a residence that would reflect his immensely powerful status as well as being opulent enough to provide suitable accommodation for visiting royalty. He therefore rebuilt Audley End as a palace fit for a king. Work on the house was finally completed in 1614 when Howard was elevated to the position of Lord Treasurer of England. When James I visited Audley End he wryly remarked that it was far too great a house for a king but might suit a Lord Treasurer. Howard's extravagant lifestyle caught up with him and he fell out of favour with the king, even spending a few days in the Tower of London under charges of corruption. He died heavily in debt and the family never recovered from his excesses.

In 1666 Charles II bought Audley End, attracted by its proximity to Newmarket racecourse, and Audley End remained a royal palace until the reign of William III

when Sir Christopher Wren advised that it would be too costly a burden for the monarchy to maintain. The king returned Audley End to the Suffolk family but the house was threatened with demolition in 1745 when Henry, 10th Earl of Suffolk, died without children and the estate was divided up. Fortunately, Audley End was bought by Elizabeth, Countess of Portsmouth, granddaughter of James, 3rd Earl of Suffolk, and she made a number of improvements to the house and gardens. On her death the estate passed to her nephew who later became Sir John Griffin Griffin, 4th Baron Howard de Walden and 1st Baron Braybrooke. He employed the architect Robert Adam and the landscape designer 'Capability' Brown to make great changes to Audley End. In the 1820s the 3rd Baron Braybrooke made further alterations creating opulent rooms in the 'Jacobean' style, and the elaborate parterre in the garden. During the Second World War Audley End served as the secret headquarters of the Polish section of the Special Operations Executive. The house was purchased for the nation in 1948 and is now in the care of English Heritage.

Abbey Lane Chapel, Saffron Walden: There has been a long history of Nonconformity in **Saffron Walden**, and there were many different groups in the town in the 1870s. After the Toleration Act of 1689 followers of the Revd Jonathan Paine began to worship regularly in a barn in Abbey Lane, and later they built their own chapel as Independents. Nonconformists such as George Gibson and John Player were generous benefactors of the town funding the Museum, Friends' School and a Teacher Training College.

Audley End Station: Situated about 1 mile from **Audley End** House on the railway line connecting Cambridge and Liverpool Street, London. The railway followed the line of valley of the River Cam but had to swerve in order to avoid Audley End. On 23 November 1863 **Saffron Walden** was linked to this railway via a branch line but this was closed in the 1960s.

Aviary: In 1774 a Menagerie was built near the Temple of Victory in the grounds of **Audley End** House. A large number of unusual and exotic birds were housed here including multi-coloured pheasants, parrots, canaries and eagles. It comprised a central Tea Room flanked by aviaries where the birds could be admired in comfort.

Babraham Hall: Situated some 7 miles from Cambridge near the Gogmagog Hills, the original Babraham Hall was one of the seats of Horatio Palavicini, the Genoese collector-general of the Papal taxes in England during the reign of Queen Mary. He was accused of embezzling money and, naturally preferring to remain in England rather than face the music back home, he became a naturalised British subject when Elizabeth I came to the throne – even commanding a warship against the Spanish in the Armada. The Hall was rebuilt in 1832 by its then owner Henry Adeane and was described as one of the finest 'modern' homes in East Anglia, with extensive and very fine gardens and parkland. At the time of the diary Charles Robert Whorwood Adeane, born 1863, had succeeded to the estate on the death of his father in 1870. Babraham Hall was destroyed by fire in the late 19th century.

Chesterford Park: An estate situated 1 mile east of the village of Little Chesterford, north of **Saffron Walden**. In 1856 it was owned by George Sandars who built a mansion incorporating the already existing farmhouse. Later owners included Mr Pickersgilt Cunliffe who reputedly invented the Cunliffe patented umbrella shooting stick. Sir James Lyle Mackay bought the estate in 1909, adopting the title of Lord Inchcape after the famous rock off the coast of Arbroath, his home town. It is now a centre for agrochemical research.

*Opposite, top left: Babraham Hall; **top right:** Church of St Andrew and St Mary, Grantchester; **centre:** Free Library, Cambridge; **below:** Crystal Palace*

Babraham Hall.

Christchurch, Sydenham: A chapel of ease to St. Mary's, Lewisham, situated on the corner of Sydenham Road and Trewsbury Road. A new church, All Saints, was founded on the site in 1901.

Crystal Palace: By 1873 at its new site at Sydenham, south London, the Crystal Palace hosted numerous exhibitions, fêtes, shows etc and people from all over the country flocked to enjoy its attractions. Such was its popularity that the railway companies organised special trains and excursions to keep up with the demand.

Ellison Road: Road in Streatham named after the Ellison family, large landowners in the area in the 18th century. Their property descended through many generations to the Crooke, Ellison and Bates Estate which survived into the 20th century. Among the earliest houses in this road are the even numbers 218–50. These artisans' dwellings were known locally as Teapot Terrace as they were said to have been built by a dedicated teetotaller.

Fishpond ground: Now known as the Pond Garden, this is situated just outside the walled Kitchen Garden at **Audley End**. It was built in 1865, inspired by the taste for rugged landscapes. An article in *The Garden*, 21 July 1877, describes how this area has 'among many other suitable wall shrubs and climbers, a specimen of a fine old evergreen Rose (*Maria Leonida*), now rarely seen; and in one of the ponds or basins are thriving examples of *Richardia aethiopica* and *Aponogeton distachyon*. The chief feature, however, in this department is a piece of artificial rockwork by Pulham, which, although it may not harmonise happily with its surroundings, nor yet, as an imitation, meet the requirements of a geologist, produces a pleasing effect; the blocks, from long exposure, are weather-stained and mossy, and the crevices are filled with the true Shamrock (*Oxalis Acetosella*), *Cotyledon umbilicus*, and the smaller-growing Ferns, &c. . . arranged and planted by someone who evidently had studied natural, or in other words, true artistic effects.'

Free Library: This was situated in the centre of Cambridge next to the Guildhall on Wheeler Street.

Grantchester: Situated some 3 miles from Cambridge, this lovely village has been associated with many famous people over the centuries. William Cresswell was born and brought up here. At that time, in the mid-19th century, the village was self supporting with a butcher, baker, tailor, shoemaker, blacksmith, brickmaker, miller, farmers and market gardeners. Most of the men worked on the land and women were employed as cooks, housemaids, or servants in the large houses in Grantchester, or as 'bedders' in the Cambridge colleges.

The Church of St Andrew & St Mary was the focus of the village. The chancel was built in the 14th century and the tower dates from the early 15th century. When the south aisle was added in 1876, evidence of a possible Saxon church on the site was discovered. The famous clock was added at around the time William Cresswell was writing his diary. It is what most people associate with Grantchester church – the lines written in 1912 by the poet Rupert Brooke wistfully recalling his happy time living at the Old Vicarage in Grantchester: 'Stands the clock at ten to three, and is there honey still for tea?'

Next to the church was the cottage where the Cresswell family lived. This had been built for the Clerk of the church after, in 1806, Mary Butts of Grantchester left £100 in her will for this purpose. The cottage cost £70 to build and the remainder of the legacy was used to finance a salary paid to the Clerk for keeping the churchyard in order. William's father, **James**, took over the cottage on his appointment as Clerk and William notes in his diary about how he helps his father in the churchyard. The cottage was demolished in 1955/6 and the new house (now the Vicarage) on the site was originally named 'Cresswell'.

Mr Hart's shop: A long-established family business in **Saffron Walden**, still trading today.

Hospital: This would be Addenbrooke's Hospital in Trumpington Road, Cambridge.

Immanuel Church: Situated on Streatham High Street, Streatham Common. By the early 1850s the population of Streatham had grown so much that the parish church of St Leonard was proving too small to accommodate everyone who wanted to attend services. So in 1854 it was decided that a new church should be

HENRY HART'S

General Printing Office,

KING   STREET,

SAFFRON   WALDEN.

Posting & Sale Bills	Tea Papers	Prospectuses
Catalogues	Direction Cards	Invoices
Billheads	Circulars	Business Cards
Particulars and Conditions of Sale	Hand Bills	Sermons
Account Book Headings	Bookwork	Tracts
	Pamphlets	Cheque Books
Drapers' Bills	Mourning Cards	Receipt Books
	Rate Books	Envelopes

AND EVERY OTHER DESCRIPTION OF LETTER-PRESS PRINTING.

PRINTING IN COLOURED INKS, GOLD,
SILVER, AND BRONZES,

IN EVERY SHADE, NEATLY EXECUTED.

Copper-plate & Lithographic Printing

ESTIMATES

carefully made at the lowest remunerative prices, and
sent free by post on application.

built and the then Rector of Streatham, the Revd John Nicholl, approached leading residents to support the venture. Andrew Hamilton donated part of his garden to build the church on, and many wealthy and influential people added their support – in particular its first two churchwardens, **William Leaf** and William M Coulthurst. Leaf lived at Park Hill, a large Georgian mansion that still survives today near the junction of Streatham Common North and Leigham Court Road; Coulthurst was a partner in Coutts Bank and was described as a 'friend of boundless generosity'. He lived at Streatham Lodge, a large mansion situated opposite Elm Lodge where William Cresswell worked.

Immanuel Church was rebuilt in 1865 to designs by the architect Benjamin Ferry and a side chapel was added in 1876 to increase seating capacity to accommodate over 1,000 people. The church's name takes the more unusual 'I' spelling and is a Hebrew word meaning 'God is with us'.

All that remains today of the old church is the tower. In 1987 the body of the church was demolished and a new church built behind the tower. The rest of the site was developed with sheltered accommodation for the elderly called St John's House – named after St John's College, Cambridge, from where Immanuel's first vicar, the **Revd Stenton Eardley**, graduated in 1846.

Littlebury: Village situated less than 1 mile from **Audley End** House with Holy Trinity Church situated on the edge of the village.

Long Stowe Hall: An ancient building and estate situated 12 miles south-west of Cambridge. It was the seat of Sidney Stanley JP and extensive additions were made in 1865–70. The house was set in a park of more than 80 acres with pleasure grounds 'well studded with timber' and extensive fish ponds.

Lord's Bridge Station: Once a station on the line from Cambridge to Bedford.

Pampisford Hall.

Newnham Croft: An area in Grantchester close to the river by the (then) boundary with Cambridge. It later became known as 'New Grantchester' and was eventually incorporated into Newnham. A house in Grantchester called Newnham Croft was listed in the 1861 census when it was occupied by the Finch family.

Norwood cemetery: This was the present-day West Norwood Cemetery. It opened in 1837 to cope with the demand for burial space caused by the rapid expansion of the suburbs. Designed by (Sir) William Tite in an informal manner with a number of deciduous trees, it soon became south London's most fashionable cemetery – popularly referred to as 'Millionaire's Cemetery' because of the number and quality of the elaborate memorials it contained. It provided a popular venue for Sunday visitors, many of whom came to admire the monuments and attractive grounds. Many famous people are buried in the cemetery including **Charles Spurgeon** and the **Revd Stenton Eardley.**

One Tree Hill: A popular part of Greenwich Park offering unparalleled views over London. The one tree was blown down in 1848. It has continued to be enjoyed as an open space after a strong public campaign resisted attempts to develop it in the 1890s.

Pampisford Hall: Mansion built in the early 19th century on a slight hill about 1 mile from Pampisford. It was renowned for its magnificent painted ceilings, the work of Italian craftsmen. The grounds contained one of the finest collections of conifers in the country including specimens from California, Japan and China; and there was a flower garden laid out in the Italian style.

Opposite, top left: Immanuel Church, Streatham; top right, Entrance to Norwood cemetery; centre left: Lord's Bridge Station; centre right: Pampisford Hall; below left: Greenwich Hospital viewed from One Tree Hill; below right: Pied Bull Inn, Streatham

Pied Bull Inn: Situated near Streatham Common, on Streatham High Road. The earliest known mention of the inn occurs in 1736 and it was probably built to provide accommodation and refreshment to people visiting the minerals wells. These had been discovered in 1659 and were situated at the top of Streatham Common in what is now known as the Rookery Gardens.

At the beginning of the 19th century, the Pied Bull was a coaching stop on the London to Brighton route where the horses were changed. In 1832 Young and Bainbridge leased the premises and it has remained in the ownership of the brewery ever since.

The Pied Bull was popular with locals and the workers at the adjacent P B Cow's factory. It was for this reason that in 1878 the **Revd Stenton Eardley** built the Beehive Coffee Tavern next to the pub to provide an alternative temperance venue for those who preferred 'the cup that cheers' rather than the strong ale and spirits on offer at the Pied Bull. Prior to this, temperance meetings had been held in an old Georgian house that occupied the site and this was where William Cresswell would have attended temperance meetings.

Reading Room: Formerly the village school in **Grantchester**, this one-roomed thatched building was used after 1867 as a meeting place for the village; it is now an extension to Grantchester Village Hall.

Riversdale: Built in **Grantchester** in 1854 by Samuel Page Widnall, who then lived at the Old Vicarage, on the site of part of his father's commercial flower nursery. In the 1870s the house was occupied by the Misses Cowlard, sisters of the **Revd William Martin's** wife. The house was much enlarged and altered in the 1900s.

Russell Street, Cambridge: Number 24 which William Cresswell refers to in his diary was the home of Thomas Blatch, a railway servant, at this period. William may have known him through his links to the **Apthorpe** family who lived in the same street.

S. Common: Streatham Common. This was just a few minutes walk from Elm Lodge where William was working at the time, and a popular area for Sunday strollers.

S. Walden: Saffron Walden, usually referred to throughout the diary as Walden. This attractive Essex market town has a long history with origins dating to the Neolithic period. The town really began to expand in the late 14th and early 15th centuries when it became a centre for the wool trade and brewing industries. A further boost to the fortunes of the town came in the Tudor period when it was discovered that the soil and climate of Walden were perfect for the growing of the autumn-flowering crocus from which saffron is obtained. Saffron was much sought after as a dye, a spice and for its medicinal properties in the treatment of jaundice, sickness and plague. Only the stigmas of the flowers provided the valuable saffron and 30,000 flowers were needed to produce just 1lb of saffron. The fields around the town were soon a beautiful shade of blue and many of the town's inhabitants became

'crokers' (saffron growers). Such was the importance of the industry that the town took the name of Saffron Walden. By the 1870s, the town was once more enjoying a period of rapid expansion with the arrival of the railways and improved road links.

Saffron Walden Common: A large open area in the town which has for many centuries been used for fairs, special events etc. At its edge is an ancient turf maze.

St Mark's church: Built in 1871 in the Newnham area in what had become known as 'New Grantchester'.

Spurgeon's Tabernacle: The famous Charles H Spurgeon was at this time pastor of the Tabernacle at Elephant & Castle, south London. He had begun his ministry at the New Park Chapel in 1853 but he proved such an inspirational preacher that his congregation

*Above: King Street, Saffron Walden, in the early 20th century, and; **opposite:** Gold Street, Saffron Walden, as it is today*

soon outgrew the premises – it was claimed that over 10,000 people would gather to hear him preach. He even used the Royal Surrey Gardens Music Hall before a new site was acquired and the Tabernacle built. Part of the appeal of the site was that it was reputedly the place where the Southwark Martyrs had been burned at the stake in 1598 for their faith. In 1898 the Tabernacle was gutted by fire but rebuilt to the same design; in May 1941 it was destroyed during a bombing raid and rebuilt to a new design.

Streatham Common Station: This was opened by the London, Brighton & South Coast Railway on 1 December 1862 when it was known as Greyhound Lane Station. When first built the station was very isolated and locals wondered why it had been erected in such a remote spot in the middle of open fields. As few travellers knew where Greyhound Lane was, the name was changed to Streatham Common Station in 1870. The original building was demolished when the present station was erected on the site in 1902.

Streatham Station: This had been opened in 1868 by the South London & Sutton Junction Railway Company. The entrance was in Station Approach and passengers were forced to use a wooden footbridge to cross the line, resulting in considerable criticism from passengers. As the number of passengers using the station increased, it was decided to construct a new station on the bridge over the railway lines with an entrance on the High Road. This was designed so that passengers could access both platforms from the booking hall, and the footbridge was demolished. The new station was finished in 1898 complete with a prestigious new entrance which was considered more in keeping with Streatham's growing importance as a select residential area. This building continued to serve local commuters until 1991 when a new station opened on the site.

Streatham Hill Church: Probably Christ Church. The foundation stone was laid on 11 August 1840 by Archdeacon Wilberforce, the son of William Wilberforce, the great anti-slavery campaigner. The church was designed in the Byzantine style by James Wild when he was only 26 years old and is widely regarded as one of his finest achievements. The design was prompted by the then Rector of Streatham, the Revd Henry Blunt, who mentioned to Wild how impressed he had been with the small 12th-century churches he had seen on a visit to Italy. The bell tower is reminiscent of St Mark's Church in Venice.

Streatham Hill Station: Opened in 1856 on the first line to reach Streatham – the West End of London & Crystal Palace Railway – in order to take passengers to and from the **Crystal Palace** in Sydenham. It was originally called Streatham Station, changing its name to Streatham and Brixton Hill in 1868 and adopting the name Streatham Hill in 1869. The original simple, single-storey wooden building remains much as it was when it was first erected and is one of the last stations of its type to survive in suburban London. It is built on the bridge over the railway lines and weight restrictions mean that a more substantial, brick-built building cannot be erected here.

Tooting Common: Tooting had been a rural district until the 18th century when many fine mansions were built around the Common by wealthy Londoners. The once extensive common land began to be divided up by roads and railways as the suburbs spread, but in the 1870s Tooting Common was still an extensive expanse of open land.

Walden church: St Mary the Virgin at **Saffron Walden** is the largest parish church in Essex. A massive Norman church was built on the site of an earlier Saxon wooden church, and enlarged in the mid-13th century. In the 15th century the church was largely rebuilt in the Perpendicular style. The elegant spire was added in 1832.

Streatham Hill Station

PEOPLE

M.A.A.: Mary Ann Apthorpe who was born in Cambridge on 2 July 1850. She was listed in the 1851 census as living with her mother Ann, elder sister Elizabeth and brother James Waterfield Apthorpe (born 6 April 1847), at 33 Staffordshire Place, Cambridge. Ten years later she and James were lodging with **Mrs Carlton**, the mother of William's girlfriend, who was probably a relative. By 1871 Mary Ann had become a milliner, perhaps helping Mrs Carlton in her business. She is often mentioned in the diary and in 1876 she and her brother were two of the witnesses to William and Eliza's wedding.

Alfred: Probably Alfred, a servant listed as working at the Vicarage, **Grantchester**.

Mrs. Apthorpe: Probably the wife of James Waterfield Apthorpe, the brother of Mary Ann Apthorpe (**M.A.A**). The Apthorpes were living at 1 Eden Street, Elm Hill in 1881 and had a 6-year-old son, James Carlton Apthorpe.

Barret: Sometimes referred to simply by the initial B, he seems to have been a gardener or labourer employed by the **Yeos**, and working with William at Elm Lodge, Streatham.

Mr Bastard: Probably John Pollexfen Bastard who was born in Totnes, Devon, in 1836. He was a carpenter and builder by trade who lived in Bakers Lane (now known as Barrow Road) and whose business premises were at one time situated at 11 Bedford Row, opposite Streatham Green.

JNO. P. BASTARD,
Carpenter & Upholsterer, House Repairs, &c.
Undertaker
To any of the Metropolitan or Provincial Cemeteries.
11, BEDFORD ROW, STREATHAM, S.W.

J. Bedgegood: James Bedgegood, labourer and garden worker, who earned 1s 10d a day in 1873 and worked in **Mr Bryan's** department in the Kitchen Garden at **Audley End**. William makes a note of his birthday on 19 July 1874 but his age is not recorded.

Lady Braybrook: Born Hon Florence Priscilla Alicia Maude on 27 October 1825 in Italy, she was the daughter of Cornwallis, 3rd Viscount Hawarden. She married Charles Cornwallis Neville, later 5th Baron Braybrooke at St James's, Westminster on 9 October 1849. They had a daughter, Augusta Neville, born in 1860. In 1881 their London home was at 42 Upper Brook Street. Lady Braybrooke died on 18 March 1914.

Lord Braybrook: Born Hon Charles Cornwallis Neville on 29 August 1823 at Waltham St. Lawrence, Berkshire, he became 5th Baron Braybrooke in 1861 on the death of his brother. He formed the Lower Gallery in 1863 by glazing in the open arcade on the east front of **Audley End** House. He died in 1902 and his younger brother, the Hon & **Revd Latimer Neville**, succeeded to the title.

Mrs Brown: One of the 'garden women' employed at **Audley End** who provided clean linen for the gardeners. In 1874 she had been working for the estate for 11 years and was between 25 and 50 years of age. She earned 11d a day in 1873.

Mr Bryan: John Bryan was in charge of the Kitchen and Flower Gardens at **Audley End** while **Mr Young** was responsible for the Pleasure Grounds. It was unusual to have two head gardeners and this probably happened because Mr Young was approaching retirement – indeed William Cresswell notes on 14 May 1874 that he has heard Mr Young is leaving.

John Bryan was born on 28 November 1834 in Stonehouse, Gloucestershire. His father was gardener for the Kerr family who lived at Hay Hill House near Newnham-on-Severn, Gloucestershire, but he was murdered in 1846 when he was attacked on his way home from market. His widow and eight children, including five-month-old twins, were looked after by the Kerrs who ensured the children received an elementary education and later employed them. As the eldest son, John Bryan received a better education than his siblings. At the age of 17 he had become a professional gardener although he was still living at home.

By 1861 he was an unmarried gardener working for William Clarke Cornwallis Neville at Heydon House in Heydon, Essex (now Cambridgeshire) who no doubt recommended him to his relative **Lord Braybrooke**. He probably arrived late 1867 as he married Sarah Elphick in London on 7 December 1867. The couple lived in the Nursery Lodge and in 1873 he is recorded as earning 27 shillings a week for being in charge of his own department. His position was one of great status on a par with the highest ranking servants in the house. The couple had three children, John (1868–1916), Sarah Ann (1870–92) and Esther (1874–1951).

On Mr Young's retirement, John Bryan negotiated a new contract and became Head Gardener for both departments. This was despite the qualms of **Lady Braybrooke** who in a letter dated 12 March 1874 says that she believes that 'Bryan (was) gradually becoming extravagant and careless like Mr Young, and of course the longer he continues to act without any proper control, the more difficult it will be to check it'. Bryan had left Audley End by 1879 as William Harrison was appointed as Head Gardener on 13 May that year. Harrison had worked at Norton Priory at Halton, Cheshire, and interestingly his reference from Sir Richard Brooke states: 'He was about 7 years at Norton Priory and was not unnecessarily extravagant.'

John Bryan moved to Alderbrook at Albury, Surrey, where he worked as a gardener and land steward; in 1891 and 1901 he was in Frimley, Surrey. By 1904 he was recorded as working and living in Camberley, Surrey. He apparently bought a pub in his retirement and in the early 20th century moved to Eastbourne where his daughter Esther lived. He died in 1911.

Mrs Buttress: The Buttresses were family friends; their birthdays are recorded in the birthday book made by William Cresswell's daughter, Susan.

E.A.C: Eliza Ann Carlton, William's girlfriend, who was born on 21 November 1848 at 7 Portland Place, Cambridge. Her father, William, was a tailor born in Great Bressingham, Norfolk in *c* 1827 but he died when Eliza was still quite young. Her mother was **Mary Ann Curry Carlton** (*née* Lingwood). By the time of the diary Eliza was a housemaid at the Vicarage in **Grantchester** working for the **Revd William Martin** and his wife Eliza. After many years of courtship, Eliza and William married in 1876. Eliza died on 1 May 1939, aged 90.

H.C.: Henry Cresswell, William's older brother. He was born in **Grantchester** in 1851 and married Fanny, who was also born in Grantchester, moving to Leyton Low in east London where he became head shopman and salesman in a seed merchant business. He died on 24 July 1884 aged only 33 and is buried next to his parents in Grantchester churchyard, alongside Fanny who died on 21 July 1891 aged 40.

Mrs. Carlton: Born in Brandon, Suffolk in *c* 1828, she married William Carlton, a tailor. On his death, she carried on his trade to support Eliza (**E.A.C.**) and her two sisters, Susannah and Caroline, and was listed in the 1861 census as being a waistcoat-maker and tailor. Mary Ann supplemented her income by taking in lodgers and in 1861 three young members of the **Apthorpe** family, who may have been relatives of the Carltons, were living with them. In 1871 she was listed as being a governess and ten years later she was living at 38 Eden Street, close to where James Waterfield Apthorpe was residing.

Mr. Chater: The Chaters may well have been family friends of the Cresswells as their name crops up regularly in the diary. Several Chater families are

WILLIAM CHATER,

Nurseryman,

AGRICULTURAL & HORTICULTURAL

SEEDSMAN,

SAFFRON WALDEN, ESSEX.

Every Article in connection with the above Business supplied at the
most reasonable price consistent with a genuine article.

PRICE LISTS UPON APPLICATION.

recorded as living in Cambridge at this time and they were employed in a variety of businesses. William is probably writing to William Chater who was born in Helions Bumpstead, Essex in *c* 1802 and who was running a thriving nursery business in **Saffron Walden**, Essex, by the 1870s. In April 1871 he is recorded as having premises in Common Road, Saffron Walden, and employing 14 men. He supplied the nearby **Audley End** estate and he may well have helped William Cresswell obtain a position there in 1874. William Chater was famous for developing the ornamental semi-double and double hollyhocks in a wide variety of hues. In 1873, the year William is writing to him, his business suffered a severe setback when a fungus disease virtually wiped out his stock. However, he managed to rebuild his stock and business which thrived until his death in 1885 when it was taken over by Messrs Webb & Brand, one of the largest of hollyhock growers in the world. Webb & Brand sold the nursery to James Vert, the Cheshire-born Head Gardener of Audley End, in 1912.

J.J. Chater: Fruit and seed merchant with premises at 9 Peas Hill, Cambridge.

Professor Clark: Professor E.C. Clark (later Regius Professor of Civil Law) lived at Grove Lodge, **Grantchester**. His children, Eddie and May, were pupils of Lally Smith, Samuel Page Widnall's sister-in-law, who ran a small school at the Old Vicarage.

William Claydon: A labourer, who earned 1s 11d a day in 1873, working primarily in **Mr Bryan's** department although he seems to have worked all over the **Audley End** estate. He may well be related to Mr and Mrs Claydon who are mentioned in the diary on 14 October 1874. In 1855 a Claydon is listed as helping with the initial preparation of the **Orchard House**.

Miss Coulthurst: Hannah Isabella (Mabella) Coulthurst was the youngest sister of William Matthew Coulthurst (*see* note on **Immanuel Church**). William was the senior partner of Coutts Bank and responsible for the bank's extensive property interests in Surbition, Surrey. He endowed the church at Surbiton with £24,000 for building and furnishing, and the dedication stone of the church is inscribed: 'A thank offering to God for blessings vouchsafed, for the faithful preaching of His Word. Also in loving memory of a much loved sister Hannah Mabella Coulthurst.'

Mr Curry: Probably a relative of **Mrs Carlton** whose name was Mary Ann Curry Carlton.

Mr Daniels: The Daniels family had lived in Streatham for generations and their name first appears in the parish rate books in 1746. Henry Daniels was sexton of the parish church of St Leonard for almost 50 years until his death at the age of 76 in 1878. His son, Henry Junior, was superintendent of Immanuel Sunday School and a keen bellringer at **Immanuel Church**. Like his father, he was a staunch teetotaller and he later became the manager of the Beehive Coffee Tavern. Another member of the family, William Daniels, was a domestic gardener who lived at 1 **Ellison Road** in South Streatham.

Revd Stenton Eardley: First vicar of **Immanuel Church**, Streatham, who served the parish from 1854–83. Born near Chapel-le-Frith, Derbyshire, in 1821, he was ordained in 1846. When he first came to Immanuel the church served the small rural hamlet of

South Streatham which mainly comprised a cluster of houses round the northern end of Greyhound Lane and a few cottages at Lower Streatham between Hermitage Lane and the River Graveney, beyond which lay open fields as far as Thornton Heath.

As the population of his parish grew, the Revd Stenton Eardley quickly adapted to changing conditions and Immanuel became known as one of the best organised parishes in the country with day and Sunday schools, district visitors, church and temperance choirs, a **band of hope**, a medical club for the poor, a building society and a temperance society.

A charismatic preacher, the Revd Stenton Eardley was a champion of the Temperance Movement for almost 25 years and was known nationally for his work. In 1879 he raised £6,000 for the building of the Beehive Coffee Tavern and Assembly Rooms which were built next to the **Pied Bull** public house in Streatham High Road. This temperance hall provided a teetotal environment in which local residents and workmen could obtain wholesome meals and entertain themselves free from the temptation of alcohol. The building survives today and is now in use as solicitors' offices. The Revd Stenton Eardley paid for the third bell in the Immanuel tower and it was named the 'total abstainer'.

He held open-air services on Streatham Common attracting thousands of worshippers; he also inspired his parishioners to build other churches – two locally in West Streatham and West Lambeth and two in Switzerland. He died in July 1883 and is buried in West **Norwood cemetery**. Eardley Road in Streatham is named after him.

F: Father. James Cresswell, who was born on 2 February 1825. His place of birth is recorded as Trumpington on the census returns but the parish records do not include his name. There is a Cresswell family in **Grantchester** at this period with records of a William Cresswell (born 8 October 1826) and Henry (born March 1828). Their parents are listed as Elizabeth and Robert Cresswell.

James Cresswell was a professional gardener who may well have worked for a time at Widnall's Nursery in **Grantchester**. This was one of the region's most successful nurseries and was renowned for developing new varieties of dahlia. For 32 years he was also the deputy Parish Clerk and Assistant Overseer to Grantchester church and was awarded an extra 5 guineas when he retired in 1903. (In 1601, every parish had to have overseers to levy and distribute the poor rate; this office was abolished in 1925). The Parish Clerk was the **Revd Francis George Howard** but this appointment was probably in name only and James Cresswell took on most of his duties. James was meticulous in his work and was a much-respected member of the community. Records describe him as a village character remembered for his silvery-grey curls, his assiduous attention in opening the door to the pulpit for the vicar and his frequent 'Amens'. He died on 16 December 1905 aged 80, and is buried in Grantchester churchyard next to his wife and eldest son.

Mr & Mrs Farrow: Probably Thomas and Fanny Farrow; Thomas was a labourer from Suffolk who lived in Brixton in the 1870s and then moved to West Streatham around 1880. They lived at Besley Street which at that time was inhabited by some of the poorest residents of Streatham. Thomas and Fanny attended **Immanuel Church** and William may well have met them there.

G: George Cresswell, William's brother, who was born *c* 1861 at **Grantchester**. In 1881 he was apprenticed to an organ builder and by 1901 he was listed as living in London and working as an organ builder.

Opposite, top left to right clockwise: John Bryan, Head Gardener at Audley End House; William Leaf of Park Hill, Streatham; The Revd Francis George Howard, Curate and Parish Clerk of Grantchester church; 'Lizzie', Susan Elizabeth Cresswell in later years; The Revd Stenton Eardley of Immanuel Church, Streatham

W. George: Probably William George of Oak Lodge, Streatham Common North, the 41-year-old manager of a wholesale flower warehouse.

Mrs. H. Glasscock: The Glasscocks were friends of the Cresswell family. A John Glasscock is recorded as being a butcher in **Grantchester** around this time.

Mrs Hall (Jane Papworth): Jonah Papworth (proprietor of houses), Margaret Papworth and their daughter lived at 73 Eden Street in 1881. This was the street where the **Apthorpes** and **Mrs Carlton** also lived.

Haggers: A hairdresser with registered premises at 15 Bridge Street, Cambridge.

Revd F.G. Howard: Francis George Howard, the youngest (and posthumous) son of one of **Grantchester's** principal farmers, and the last of a number of generations of Howards in the village. After graduating at Trinity College, Cambridge, he became Curate of Grantchester church, and also Chaplain of his college. By 1873 he had undertaken another responsibility, becoming Chaplain of Non-Collegiate Students, a post which developed into that of Censor. Thus he became Head of what was to be known as Fitzwilliam House (later Fitzwilliam College) in Cambridge, moving into the town on the death of his mother. These responsibilities gave him little time for other duties and so his position of Parish Clerk of Grantchester church must have been mainly honorary, in token of his strong attachment to the place of his birth. Most of the responsibilities of Parish Clerk would have fallen on **James Cresswell**, William's father.

Johnny: John Cresswell, one of William's younger brothers. Born around 1864 at **Grantchester**, he was living at home with his parents in Church Cottage and apprenticed to a piano tuner at the time William was writing his diary. By 1901 he was a professional piano tuner.

W.L.: William Leaf, a wealthy silk merchant and banker living in Streatham. He was born in 1791 and married his cousin, Jane Leaf, in 1815. They had 11 children. In 1830 he employed John Papworth to design him a magnificent mansion on the site of an existing house in Streatham which had originally been known as Hill House. The new mansion was called Park Hill and still survives today. The surrounding grounds covered more than 17 acres and included a large ornamental lake, a grotto and a kitchen garden. William Leaf also had a mock medieval castle built as an ornamental garden feature and observation point from where he could admire the surrounding countryside. This was one of the finest gardens in Streatham and it was not surprising that, on the day he received his notice from the Yeos, William aspired to a position at Park Hill.

U. Lamb: Uncle Lamb. In 1881 Anne Richmond Lamb was living with the **Apthorpe** family in Eden Street, Cambridge. She was listed as a cousin and was born *c* 1866 in London. Her father, James Lamb, was a railway worker living in 1871 at 145 Healey Street, Marylebone. His wife Eliza was born in Brandon, Suffolk – the same place as **Mrs Mary Ann Carlton** was born. It is likely that Eliza and Mary Ann were sisters.

Lizzie: Susan Elizabeth Cresswell, William's sister, who was born at **Grantchester** in 1857. Her name appears frequently in the diary and William is obviously very fond of her. He records her appointment as a nursery nurse in 1874, and by 1881 she had become a housemaid at the Vicarage in Grantchester, perhaps taking **Eliza Carlton's** place. She later became a teacher and married Thomas Lane. Lizzie died on 13 April 1936.

Opposite, top left: Park Hill, Streatham; *top right*: The Vicarage, Grantchester; *centre left*: Willers Nursery, Cambridge – note the advertisement for canary guano; *centre right and below*: Interior and exterior of Grantchester Mill

Miss Lloyd: Frances and Eliza Lloyd were two spinster sisters who ran a 'superior ladies' school' at Streatham Court, a large house that stood on the southern junction of Streatham Common South and the High Road. At this time there were some 19 pupils at the school ranging in age from 6 to 19, including Amy Lloyd, the sisters' 14-year-old niece. The school had been established in 1860 and continued until the death of Frances in 1892.

Mr Lowe: George Lowe was a miller working at Grantchester Mill which was managed by the Nutter family. He lived in a house attached to the mill but, when a fire destroyed the mill in 1928, he set up as a carpenter in the village.

Revd Mr Chas Loxley: Chaplain of King's College, Cambridge. He lived in Merton Cottage in **Grantchester** for a few years.

Lyles & Speed: A prestigious nursery and seed merchant in Cambridge listed in *Spalding's Directory* of 1875 as having premises at 15 Alexandra Street near Petty Cury.

LYLES & SPEED,
NURSERYMEN,
AGRICULTURAL & HORTICULTURAL
SEEDSMEN & FLORISTS,
GONVILLE NURSERY,
AND
The Royal Cambridgeshire Seed Establishment,
15, PETTY CURY,
CAMBRIDGE.

Every effort made to supply the best of everything.

Revd W. Martin: Born *c* 1819 at **Littlebury**, Essex, he became Vicar of **Grantchester** in 1850. Finding that the old 17th-century vicarage was in a poor state of repair, he had a new Vicarage built in the centre of the village. The freehold of the Old Vicarage was bought by Samuel Page Widnall. Both Cresswell's sister **Lizzie** and his girlfriend **Eliza Carlton** worked for the Revd William Martin at the Vicarage. He died on 5 July 1882. His wife was born Eliza Cowlard in *c* 1819 at Thorverton, Devon. On her husband's death she moved away from Grantchester to live in Bournemouth.

Mother: Susan Cresswell, born 23 March 1823 at Horningsea, Cambridgeshire. She was the daughter of Sarah and John Holmes, and her father was a cordwainer (shoemaker) by profession. Susan Cresswell died on 25 June 1894 and is buried in **Grantchester**.

Mr Moule: Ebenezer Moule was born *c* 1832 in **Saffron Walden**. In 1871 was living in the Garden Lodge at **Audley End** with his wife Charlotte. In 1873 he was listed as a gardener working in **Mr Young's** department and earning 2s 4d. When Mr Young left in 1874, Moule was given a new contract from **Mr Bryan** under which he was not allowed to sell garden produce from his garden – but his wage was increased to £1 14s a week, as well as £2 when he needed to attend to the floodgates. By 1881 he was living in London Road, **Littlebury**, and by 1891 he was still listed as an under gardener/domestic servant.

Mr Mudd: The Curator of the Cambridge Botanic Gardens who lived at 4 College Terrace, Hills Road, Cambridge. He had been appointed Curator in 1864 on the death of the previous Curator, James Stratton. Mudd had obtained his horticultural training in the north of England and was largely self-educated in botany. He had a keen interest in lichens publishing the *Manual of British Lichens* in Darlington in 1861. Ill health restricted his career in Cambridge; he died in 1879.

Revd Latimer Neville: Born on 22 April 1827, he was the younger brother of the 4th and 5th Barons Braybrooke. He was Master of Magdalene College, Cambridge, which had been refounded by Sir Thomas Audley in the 16th century. (The Neville family still appoint the Master of Magdalene College.) In 1902, at the age of 75, he succeeded to the title as 6th Baron Braybrooke and his son Henry Neville (1855 – 1941) became 7th Baron Braybrooke on the death of his father two years later.

James Richardson: He was born *c* 1814 at nearby **Littlebury** and had already served 32 years in the **Audley End** estate by 1874. In 1873 he was earning 2s 2d a day in **Mr Young's** department. By 1881 he was living with his wife Anne and son Ralph in **Littlebury** and was still judged fit enough to be employed as an agricultural labourer.

Mr Ridnor: Thomas Ridnor, a local butcher whose shop was situated at 10 Bedford Row, opposite Streatham Green. Ridnor's man was probably one of his two assistants, Robert Large or William Jewers, who were both 19 years of age.

W. Rollisson & Sons Nursery: Springfield Nursery, Upper Tooting, was one of the most important nurseries of its kind in London in the 19th century. In 1803 William Rollisson established a nursery on land that had been owned by his father. It was situated on some of the most fertile soil in the parish with a guaranteed water supply piped from Beck spring and the Bottomless Pit spring (both of these lay in the area of Hebdon Road and were not far from the glasshouses sited where the houses of Moffat and Hereward Roads now are).

Right, top: Cucumbers were widely grown in the Victorian period and many wealthy people had special cucumber houses in their gardens; right: A wide variety of cucumbers were available – Rollisson's 'Telegraph' cucumber was particularly popular

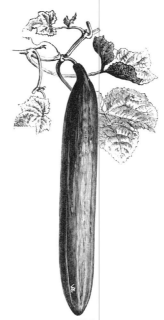

62022.
Concombre vert long Rollisson's Telegraph.
Cucumber, green long Rollisson's Telegraph.
Gurke, Rollisson's Telegraph, grüne sehr lange.
Fr. 6 30 — 5 —

William Rollisson quickly established a reputation for raising camellias from seed and in 1822 was reported as also having 'the best collection of ericae in the vicinity of the metropolis'. In the 1830s Rollisson won many prizes for rare plants and orchids and in 1851 was famous for the raising of pitcher plants. His nursery grew in size from the original 2 acres to about 45 acres by the late 1830s. After his death in 1842, the business was carried on by his son George and by the 1850s he was employing 43 men on a site that had now grown to 62 acres. The firm continued to flourish until George's death in 1880. A few years later the land was built over save for an area now used as Fishponds Road sports field.

JAMES SANDAVER,
✲ BOOT & SHOE MAKER, ✲
CROYDON ROAD, LOWER STREATHAM.

Ready-Made Goods of Every Description kept in Stock.

Repairs Neatly Executed on the shortest notice.

Mrs Sandaver: This was probably Emma Sandaver, the wife of James Sandaver, the local bootmaker who lived at 1 Orchard Place, one of a row of small cottages which were located on the western side of the High Road to the south of the **Pied Bull**. James was born in Streatham in 1825 and was the Parish Clerk at **Immanuel Church**. William records receiving a new pair of boots from Mr Sandaver on 6 September 1873 at a cost of 14 shillings.

Mr. Speed's Gonville Nursery, Cambridge: One of the nurseries of **Lyles & Speed**.

Veitch's Nursery: Originally founded in Exeter by John Veitch, a Scottish gardener, who was one of the first men to pioneer plant exploration to all corners of the world. Members of the Veitch family were among the brave plant hunters who often risked their lives in search of rare plants and seeds. In 1853 John Veitch bought a nursery in Chelsea which was run by his son James Junior, while his father remained at the original business he had founded in Exeter.

Miss Whitehead: Probably Selina Whitehead whose marriage to George Dasley is recorded later in the diary on 5 October 1874.

Willers: A nursery on the Trumpington Road, Cambridge.

Mr Yeo: William's employer when the diary opens. The Yeos lived at Elm Lodge in Streatham. Robert Yeo was born near Exeter, Devon, in 1810 and moved to Streatham around 1864 with his young wife Mary who was 30 years his junior. This was probably his second marriage as his daughter Anne Maria, aged 22, was married in Streatham's parish church of St Leonard on 18 February 1865. In 1866 Robert and Mary had a son, Gerald, whose death in June 1874 is mentioned later in William's diary.

Robert Yeo was a builder by profession but he had retired by the time William was working for him. Elm Lodge was described in 1823 as a 'handsome house' with tall, red-plastered walls and heavy plastered doorway pillars. The building was later known as Delves House and it was demolished around 1907.

Mr Young: George Young was born in Scotland in *c* 1798. As Head Gardener of the Pleasure Grounds at **Audley End**, he is recorded as being paid £80 a year plus fuel. In 1871 he, and his wife Mary-Anne aged 71, were living in the Gardener's House with their granddaughter Selina aged 17. He seems to have worked at Audley End for many years and retired in 1874.

MISCELLANEOUS

Annual tea: This was a major undertaking for **Immanuel Church** which had a large Sunday School. By the early 1880s 420 children were on the roll and there were 24 teachers.

Band of Hope: Temperance organisation for working-class children founded in Leeds in 1847. Children as young as six were enrolled in local groups, and a strong emphasis was placed on music and singing. Although the children were expected to listen to lectures on the evils of drink, they also had the opportunity to enjoy a range of activities as well as regular treats such as excursions to the seaside.

Boat race: The 31st race in 1874 resulted in the fifth win in a row for the Light Blues. Oxford had led for part of the race but were eventually beaten by 3¹/₂ lengths.

Coffee house: Established to provide accommodation and refreshments for teetotallers so that they did not have to go into hotels or inns serving alcohol.

Cricket: Charles Neville, 5th Baron **Braybrooke** was particularly interested in cricket. He laid out the cricket pitch in front of the house in 1842. In 1859 Saffron Walden Cricket Club was formally established although cricket had been played on **Saffron Walden Common** since the early years of the 19th century. Audley End Cricket Club still play on the lawn outside the main entrance.

Croquet party: Croquet reputedly started in Ireland in the 1830s and its popularity spread to England during the 1850s. It was a very social sport being the first time that women could participate in an outdoor sport on an equal basis to men, and wealthy Victorians began to ensure that a croquet lawn was included in the garden design for their homes. In 1865 Walter Whitmore-Jones of Chastleton House, Oxfordshire,

had his rules of the game published, and three years later he won the first championship at Evesham. The same year, 1868, the Wimbledon All England Croquet Club was founded as the first national headquarters.

Fire engine: A horse-drawn fire engine supplied to **Audley End** House in April 1843 by the London company of Merryweather & Sons at a cost of £299. Manned by estate workers and originally housed in the carriage house, it still survives.

Foresters Fete: The Ancient Order of Foresters is a friendly society which is still in existence. In Victorian times they held large rallies like the one in 1859 described in the *Illustrated London News*: 'On Tuesday morning some thousands of the followers of "Bold Robin Hood" treated themselves to an official visit to the Crystal Palace. The extraordinary appearance of the men as they passed through the streets of London attracted much attention. Many of the leaders were dressed in cocked hats, green coats, and stage boots, while many of them wore on their backs a singular

Enjoying a game of croquet on the lawn outside the main entrance of Audley End House

The Greyhound public house in Streatham where Miss Mackley celebrated her wedding

preparation of sheepskin, to indicate that they were 'shepherds', a title of honour conferred upon those who have passed through the principal offices of the order, such as 'woodwards,' 'rangers,' &c. . . As many as 63,181 persons were present, the largest number, we believe, ever assembled at Sydenham in one day.'

Grand fete and Gala of Ancient Shepherds: The Ancient Order of Shepherds was a friendly society which provided insurance in case of sickness or death.

Grand wedding: Amelia Mackley, widow of a merchant, Thomas Cole Mackley, lived at Ferndale, a house on the western side of the High Road, Streatham, opposite Coulthurst Cottages. Her youngest daughter, Louisa Kate, was 18 at this time. As no record of the marriage appears in the registers of **Immanuel Church**, it may be that she was married elsewhere and the celebration for her wedding held at the Greyhound.

Great Temperance Fete: Event attracting thousands of people from temperance organisations all over the country; choirs and bands would compete for prizes.

Hanging: The Victorians had a fascination with death – even organising excursions to visit the scenes of murders. A murder case known as the Whitechapel Road Mystery gripped the nation for several weeks from 12 September 1875 after a hansom cab crossing over London Bridge was stopped by police and found to contain the mutilated body of a young woman. The two people in the cab, Henry Wainwright (a 36-year-old brush manufacturer) and Alice Day (a 20-year-old ballet girl from the Pavilion Theatre), were arrested and charged with murder although they both denied the charge. The police had been alerted by an employee of Wainwright who had been told by Wainwright to help him move two heavy parcels from his business premises. They hauled the parcels onto the street and, while Wainwright went off in search of a cab, the employee decided to have a peek into one of the parcels. He was horrified to be confronted by a severed human head and quickly sealed up the parcel before Wainwright returned with the cab. They put the parcels into the cab and Wainwright went off in it, closely followed on foot by his employee to see where it went. The cab paused to pick up Alice Day and then continued on its way until Wainwright's employee eventually persuaded a couple of constables of his incredible story.

The murdered woman was finally identified as Harriet Louisa Lane, who lived with Henry Wainwright and their two children in Chingford, Essex. It emerged during the court case that Harriet had left the children with a neighbour and never returned – Wainwright claiming she had run off with another man. However Harriet's family had their suspicions – especially as Wainwright had frequently been seen in the company of Alice Day. On 2 December Henry Wainwright, still maintaining his innocence of the murder, was found guilty and sentenced to be hanged; the jury believed Alice Day when she said she knew nothing of the murder or the contents of the parcels, and she was acquitted. Wainwright was hanged in the early morning of 21 December at the Old Bailey in front of a small selected crowd of spectators.

Lecture: This probably took place in the large Georgian house next to the **Pied Bull** in which the temperance movement based at **Immanuel Church**, Streatham, met before the building of the Beehive Coffee Tavern. The lecture was obviously inspiring as William signs the pledge the next day.

Penny readings: Parochial entertainments of music, readings, etc which charged a penny entry fee to raise money, often for the Sunday School.

Regent's Canal explosion: Laden with sugar, nuts, petroleum and gunpowder, the barge *Tilbury* was being towed up the Regent's Park Canal in the early hours of Friday, 2 October 1874, when a spark ignited the gunpowder. The huge explosion that resulted caused the deaths of four people, blew up the Macclesfield Bridge and smashed windows more than a mile away. It almost completely destroyed the house of the famous artist Lawrence Alma-Tadema. There was so much chaos and confusion after the explosion that a detachment of Horse Guards was sent to keep order and ensure that no wild animals escaped from the Regent's Park Zoo and went on the rampage. It was claimed to be the largest peacetime explosion in the country.

Signing the pledge: In 1832 Joseph Livesey, a cheesemaker in Preston, Lancashire, and seven other local working men signed a pledge that they would never drink alcohol again. Three years later the British Association for the Promotion of Temperance was founded in Preston and the movement quickly spread across the country. Originally it was just opposed to drinking spirits but by the 1840s it was advocating teetotalism.

Volunteers on common: As a result of a dangerously deteriorating relationship with France, volunteer corps were created throughout the country. **Saffron Walden's** volunteer corps was gazetted on 23 October 1860 as 17 Company, Saffron Walden of the Essex Volunteer Rifle Corps with the Hon Charles C Neville (who became **Lord Braybrooke** the following year) as its Captain. In the 1870s the Essex Volunteer Companies were reorganised as 17 Company Saffron Walden and became part of the 2nd Battalion of the Essex Regiment.

The effect of the Regent's Park Canal explosion

The *Kitchen Garden*
at Audley End

The changing fortunes of the garden and how
Cresswell's diary was the key to its restoration.

FROM THE 18TH CENTURY ONWARDS, the walled kitchen garden was an essential part of every English country house. It had to provide a continual supply of fresh fruit, vegetables and flowers for the family and servants but, while meeting these demands, it was far more than merely an efficient centre of production. The essence of the walled kitchen garden lay in the quality and range of its produce – choice fruit and vegetables had to be provided for the owner's dining table at a peak of perfection and through all seasons of the year. Before the modern era of international imports and the freezer, the gardeners were expected to provide strawberries from March and salads throughout the year. Besides food, large quantities of special flowers and plants were produced for the pleasure gardens and the house. The kitchen garden was also a prized possession in its own right, regularly visited by the owner, his family and guests.

Forced on by such demands, the kitchen garden became the focus for extraordinary levels of ingenuity, skill and sheer hard work. In 1900 a leading authority could declare: 'In no country in the world are grapes grown with so much care, and brought to such perfection, as in Great Britain.' The craft of horticulture reached its apogee in these gardens.

The Kitchen Garden at Audley End House was established on its present site in the 1750s by Elizabeth, Countess of Portsmouth. Previously, the kitchen garden had been closer to the house, but as formal gardens gave way to sweeping parkland, most kitchen gardens were moved to a more discreet location. As the famous landscape gardener Humphry Repton advised in 1795, 'the true situation for a kitchen garden should be near the stables for the sake of the manure, and as near the house as possible without being seen from it'. A plan of 1758 shows the Countess of Portsmouth's new Kitchen Garden with a large

Opposite: The Vinery range at Audley End House still produces choice grapes; page 140: The Kitchen Garden at Audley End

walled enclosure of about 3 acres (1.2 hectares), divided by paths into six rectangular compartments.

In 1762 Sir John Griffin Griffin, the nephew of the Countess, inherited Audley End and soon began improving the Kitchen Garden by making a large extension to the west in 1769. He built a variety of new glasshouses, of which several fine drawings survive in the Audley End archives. A wide variety of produce could now be grown including pineapples, oranges, grapes and peaches. The grandest structure was a 'Greenhouse with flanking Hot Houses', designed by John Hobcroft and built in 1774–6. The classical design of the Greenhouse, with its tall windows, gauged brick arches and slate roof, is unusual for a kitchen garden and reminiscent of late 17th-century orangeries, before the introduction of glazed roofs. It was later replaced by the current Vinery range, and only part of its back wall now remains.

Below: John Hobcroft's design for a 'Greenhouse with flanking Hot Houses'
Opposite: *The Greenhouse was replaced by the Vinery range*

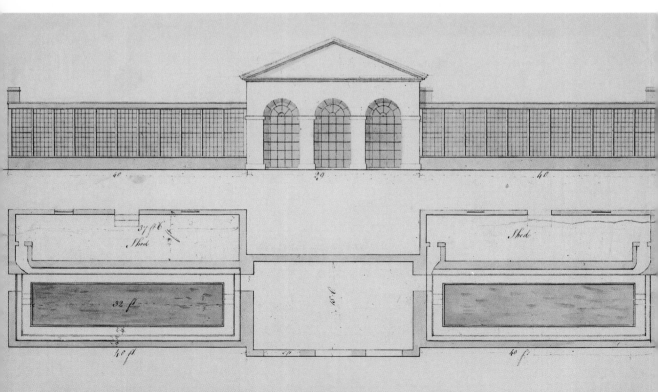

Further developments took place in the early 19th century. In 1802 the whole long west wall of the main compartment was rebuilt as a 'hot wall', incorporating extensive flues which were heated by stoke holes at regular intervals to the rear. The fires were lit at particular times for frost protection and early ripening. Hot walls were popular in the late 18th and early 19th centuries, especially for reliable production of peaches and nectarines. By Cresswell's time, however, the hot wall at Audley End had fallen out of favour.

In the 1820s the current Vinery and Backsheds range was built, replacing the earlier Greenhouse. This fine building, 170 feet (52 metres) in length, had five separate compartments to provide a variety of growing conditions for different plants. In the centre was a showhouse for flowering plants with vineries to each side and peach houses at each end. A full range of backsheds to the rear housed the furnace, potting shed, tool

store and mushroom house as well as the Bothy where William Cresswell later lived. Additional walls were built at this period to enclose further compartments, the garden growing to reach a size of over 8 acres (3.2 hectares). The Head Gardener's house was built into the south-east corner of the garden, well-placed to keep a close eye on the workforce.

The later 19th century saw rapid improvements in kitchen gardens with the introduction of hot-water boilers for heating and extensive glasshouse building. By the end of the century the gardener had at his command a wide variety of glass structures in which he could control with precision the conditions to suit fruit and vegetables, plants and flowers from all over the world.

THE KITCHEN GARDEN IN WILLIAM CRESSWELL'S DAY

A description of the Kitchen Garden at Audley End House in *The Gardeners' Chronicle* of 6 September 1884 (just 10 years after William Cresswell left) gives a very clear picture of the garden in which William spent his days:

> *As might be supposed in a place of such long standing, the means provided for the supplying of vegetables, fruit, and flowers, are in proper harmony with its extensiveness. Well formed kitchen gardens of 8½ acres, in three compartments, all furnished with excellent walls for fruit culture, and these having a great variety of aspect, from the irregular form the gardens partake. The Apricot, Peach, Nectarine, and Plum, among stone fruit, do very well on this soil, and many good trees are to be found of these. Mr. Vert, the talented young gardener, is now doing his best to completely furnish the walls with the best of old and new varieties, of all such kinds as require such assistance to ripen their fruit. The hardy fruit supplies are supplemented by an orchard-house 90 feet long*

Opposite: Fruit trees are still grown in pots in the Orchard House just as they were in William Cresswell's time

Figs ripening in the Orchard House

by 20 feet wide. In this were found many kinds of Peaches, Nectarines, Plums, Figs, mostly in pots sunk in beds of soil or else planted out. Only the best sorts were seen, and all were well burdened with fruit.

An early vinery, containing plants of Black Hamburgh and Gros Maroc; a Muscat vinery, with Bowood, Ryton, and Alexandria Muscat Grapes; a late house planted with Lady Downe's, Madresfield Court, and Black Alicante; and a cool greenhouse, planted with Black Hamburgh Grapes only, complete the tale of the Grape-houses. In addition are two Peach-houses of 36 feet in length each, and about 2600 Strawberries, of the usually approved kinds, are being grown.

The floral department receives much attention, as we saw about 600 well grown Chrysanthemums, in 250 varieties, in their flowering pots, the plants bushy, and of the healthiest appearance. These Mr. Vert will form into loosely trained natural bushes after moderate disbudding. Many Primula sinensis and P. alba plena; Salvias, such as gesneriflora, S. pseudo-coccinea, the Pine-apple perfumed sort; S. fulgens, S. Betheli, S. Bruanti, and S. Pitcherii, are grown for autumn and winter uses. A stove contained a collection of the pick of the Crotons and Dracaenas, nice stuff, fit for all those varied uses in domestic decoration for which they are so suitable. A new stove to contain these plants . . . is being built. It is a pleasing, light building, having heated beds at the sides, and a bench in the centre, under which are two narrow troughs the length of the house, which, when kept full of water, will afford a ready means of watering.

The different ranges of pits, fruit-rooms, Mushroom-houses, sheds, young men's domicile, &c, together with an extensive nursery and orchard, make the garden appointments both appropriate and very complete at Audley End.

LATER HISTORY AND DECLINE

The Kitchen Garden at Audley End seems to have reached its high point in the late 19th century. In the Edwardian period the house was leased and the 7th Baron Braybrooke, who lived here up to the Second World War, made few changes. The garden continued to operate and a number of functional new glasshouses were added during these decades but, unlike most other country house kitchen gardens in this period, there was no sweeping programme to replace the glasshouses with the latest technology at Audley End. As a result, the

The Backsheds prior to restoration

Vinery/Backsheds range survived, one of the best-preserved early 19th-century complexes of its type in the country.

The final years of the Kitchen Garden were remembered by the 7th Baron Braybrooke's daughter, the Hon Mrs Catherine Ruck, who herself worked in the garden in the early years of the Second World War and provided valuable information for the restoration. During the war, only the Little Vinery continued to be heated, but here fine white Muscat grapes were grown. Wartime restrictions prescribed that cucumbers could be produced but melons were forbidden as a luxury. Mrs Ruck recalled how melon production managed to continue – the gardeners hung up cucumbers among the melons in the melon house – and inspectors turned a blind eye.

After the Second World War, hundreds of walled kitchen gardens around the country were lost to redevelopment or neglect. But Audley End House passed into the ownership of the nation, and the continuation of the garden as a market garden business managed to preserve much of its character.

RESTORATION OF THE KITCHEN GARDEN

Restoration work started in the early 1990s with the repair of the Vinery range. With the growth of interest in kitchen gardens, this had been recognised for what it was – an extraordinarily complete early survival. Repair work came only just in time to save it as it was in an advanced state of decay. The whole structure was taken down piece by piece and painstakingly restored, saving the maximum amount of original timber.

The market garden business closed in 1998 and English Heritage took over the garden. A special partnership was formed with HDRA (now Garden Organic) to restore the site as a working organic kitchen garden. The main focus was on the

Opposite, top: The derelict Vinery range as it was in the late 1980s before restoration; below: As the old market garden was cleared, the original layout of the Kitchen Garden began to be revealed

historic core of the garden, the 2-acre compartment in front of the Vinery. Intensive research was undertaken to establish the history of the Kitchen Garden, until then a neglected part of the Audley End estate. William Cresswell's diary, donated to English Heritage five years earlier, suddenly became a document of major importance – a unique source for bringing the history of the garden to life. Other early documents, historic maps and estate bills were analysed to piece together the story. Finally, work on site got underway in January 1999.

Paths and structure

Below, left: Laying the paths with hoggin; right: Traditional box hedging was planted along the edges of the paths

The whole area was cleared of the remains of planting from the market garden era. Archaeological excavation revealed the base layers of the rectangular path layout, as indicated on historic maps. The paths were restored, dividing the garden into its original rectangular beds or 'quarters' as they were known.

One of the wonderful things about restoring a kitchen garden is that the Victorian experts wrote weighty textbooks, such as Thompson's *The Gardener's Assistant,* with detailed instructions on every aspect. For paths, Thompson prescribes the relative widths, the material to use, path-edgings and even the precise cross-camber for effective drainage.

Espaliered fruit trees once again line each 'quarter' of the Kitchen Garden

The paths were re-laid in a matching hoggin material, a mixture of gravel and clay. This is a tricky material to get right. As Thompson said:

> *Fine binding gravel is not easily obtained in some parts. Walks are sometimes objectionable from the surface consisting of gravel too sandy, and hence loose and shifting under foot, not possessing binding qualities; sometimes, on the contrary, the gravel is too loamy, and binds very firmly in dry weather but becomes very soft and cloggy in wet.*

The material for Audley End was carefully selected after samples and trials. But halfway through the work, because of February frosts, the local quarry supplier moved to a different part of the quarry and the material supplied, after being laid, turned out to be far too loose. The solution eventually found was to re-do the top layer, mixing in a clay-rich addition – an awkward process but very successful in the end. The path edgings were formed in traditional box using over 8,000 plants. With careful trimming, these have now grown on to form the attractive miniature hedges which are such a characteristic feature of many kitchen gardens.

Evidence showed that each 'quarter' had been lined with espalier-trained fruit trees and so a new framework of iron posts and wire was designed based on illustrations in Victorian catalogues, with a comprehensive planting of period apples and pears. Other details, such as the boot-scrapers for each 'quarter', were carefully copied from other examples at Audley End.

The walls required an extensive programme of repairs. A conservative approach was taken to ensure the survival of the patina of old brick surfaces, pitted by centuries of nails for trained fruit, by using carefully matched handmade bricks and lime mortar pointing. Timber doors and gates – an essential feature of every kitchen garden – were copied from the last surviving examples, painted a charcoal grey to match the original estate colour and re-fitted to openings.

Buildings

The Vinery range, repaired earlier, was now refurbished and brought back into full use. A characteristic feature of these early glasshouses is the great sliding sashes for ventilation in the roof, before the Victorians introduced cast-iron cranking systems. The design of the ones at Audley End is very ingenious as the sashes slide on small brass rollers, carried on oak runners. Each detail had to be carefully restored in the repairs. The sashes are operated by pulling on the sash cords which are counterbalanced by heavy lead weights. On 15 May 1874 Cresswell noted that: 'Cord on light in green house (the central compartment of the Vinery) broke in evening; put new one to it.' It has to be admitted that the system is awkward to use and the great sashes often stick. It is easy to see why the Victorians felt they could improve on it.

Sadly, the Little Vinery range (known to Cresswell as the late or second vinery) had become ruinous, with only the back wall remaining. It stands just outside of the main restored compartment, so it was felt appropriate that it should just be carefully preserved in its current state of romantic decay.

Opposite:
The exterior and interior of the Vinery range in the late 1980s. Restoration saved this unique building just in time

During repairs details of the old heating system came to light, a furnace with flues winding across the back wall.

A remarkable tale of restoration relates to the Orchard House, which is frequently mentioned by William Cresswell. The orchard house was a special type of glasshouse invented by the famous Victorian horticulturalist Thomas Rivers. It was devised for the efficient production of stone fruit, especially peaches and nectarines, grown as dwarf trees in pots to Rivers' special method. Research for the project had found accounts for the construction of an orchard house at Audley End in 1856, but only the brick base remained. Without any surviving evidence for its restoration, it was at first left simply as a gravelled area for standing plants out in pots. Then an extraordinary discovery was made. Terence Read, a specialist nurseryman who had been supplying period varieties of fruit for the project, happened to own a copy of Rivers' book *The Orchard House*. Turning over its pages one evening, he was amazed to find that the Audley End Orchard House was described there in detail, and there were even two drawings of it. Rivers used his book, which ran into 19 editions, to promote successful recent examples of orchard houses. The Audley End Orchard House, by happy coincidence, just happened to appear in the 11th edition of 1860 – the one which Terence Read owned.

Armed with this new information, an authentic reconstruction of the Orchard House was now possible. It made an impressive addition to the Kitchen Garden. However, its construction was not altogether straightforward – the structure as designed by Rivers seemed very slight to the team of carpenters and, while they were building, it needed an extensive set of props to hold it up. This was the time, early in 2001, when the Millennium Bridge had just been opened across the River Thames, earning itself the nickname of the 'wobbly bridge' before it had to close. It was feared the Orchard House would turn out to be the 'wobbly glasshouse'! But, trusting to Rivers' design, the work was taken forward. With the addition of iron straps of the traditional type and the final glazing, the props were finally taken away, and the Orchard House has stood firm ever since. As Rivers said of it in 1860: 'This is really a noble orchard house, and forms a healthy and most agreeable promenade.'

One of the last areas to be restored was the 1820s range of Backsheds, behind the Vinery. Here the whole range of buildings in which William Cresswell worked has been brought back into use. Most atmospheric perhaps is the potting shed with its long bench in front of the window, tall racks filled with clay pots of all sizes, and its brick floor, deeply worn by generations of gardeners.

Another unexpected discovery was the boiler-house pit at the centre of the range. This had been filled in after the Second

The restored Orchard House at Audley End

World War with a concrete floor over the top. The intention had been to use the space as a gardener's messroom, but before fitting it out it was decided that a brief check should be made on what lay under the concrete floor. As the small trial-hole got larger and larger, an incredible survival was gradually revealed. The boiler pit turned out to be a full 8 feet (2.4 metres) deep. It contained the lower parts of two boilers, complex structures of brickwork with cast-iron pipes and doors. Further investigation showed that these were examples of the well-known Weeks's 'Upright Tubular' boilers, popular from the mid-19th century. These boilers had been the 'engine room' of the whole great Vinery range, supplying all the varied demands for heating, and would have been very well known to Cresswell. The gardeners would have been expected to maintain each glasshouse to within 2°F of the desired temperature, stoking the boiler last thing every night. It was clear that the boiler pit

*Below, left: The boiler house with the mid-20th century concrete floor; **right:** When the concrete floor was removed, the 19th-century boilers were revealed*

could not be filled in again – the messroom would have to go elsewhere!

The restoration of the Bothy, where William Cresswell lived, was one of the most enjoyable parts of the project. The Bothy, situated at the end of the Backsheds range, consists of three rooms: a kitchen/living room and two bedrooms. It was agreed that it would be best to minimise the impact of repairs here, leaving the old paintwork untouched to retain the patina of hard use. But it was decided that a miniature display would be worthwhile to bring Cresswell's little bedroom to life. An expedition around the local junk shops provided the necessary simple furniture. The Project Team had fun picking out details from the diary and leaving clues around the room: the box Cresswell packed his things away in when he left Audley End; the vignette photo he was sent of his sister, Lizzie; a song-book; and other purchases he made of a black neck-tie, collar and cuffs. Finally, a key was even found for Cresswell's watch, which he seemed in the habit of losing!

Planting and horticulture

The restored main garden compartment, stretching out extensively in front of the great Vinery range and full of intensively managed planting, makes a splendid sight. Period varieties of plants have been used wherever possible, with a cut-off date of around 1900. The large central 'quarters' have four vegetable beds for crops in rotation, with crops grown in the very long rows typical of the period. Other areas are used for soft fruit and currants. Using their Heritage Seed Library and other sources, Garden Organic have built up stocks of many rare period varieties, such as the purple-podded pea and crimson-flowered broad bean. The smaller side borders have more special crops, such as saladings and herbs, as well as some of the once-common period plants such as sea kale, skirret and cardoons.

The central axis path has block planting of peonies and irises either side for cut flowers, making an impressive show in season.

The garden walls and the wire espalier structures around the 'quarters' are clothed in trained fruit – over 50 varieties of apples and 40 sorts of pear, as well as plums, cherries and apricots. Trees are trained in a wide variety of historic patterns, with fans, cordons, espaliers and palmettes. Fruit varieties reflect the local traditions of the area, in particular many from the famous Rivers nursery in nearby Hertfordshire, now lost. In the Orchard House, the gardeners are following the original orchard house techniques developed by Rivers. Peaches, nectarines and other fruit are grown in pots, and kept to dwarf size by annual root pruning. In the Vinery range, the gnarled old vines, planted 90 years ago, have gradually been brought back into shape, with a standard trained up each long rafter and laterals across the horizontal wires. The early vinery has Black Hamburg and the late house Lady Downe's Seedling, both varieties which grew here in Cresswell's time. Each winter the vines are untied and lowered from the roof supports, to encourage new growth to sprout evenly. On the back wall of the two vineries, strawberries are once again forced in pots, set high up on shelving. The central showhouse (the Greenhouse of Cresswell's day) is filled with fine floral displays, set up on pyramidal staging.

Above, left: Colourful swathes of irises flank the central path; centre: Careful pruning is required to maintain the health of the ancient vines; right: Sea kale is just one of the more unusual vegetables now thriving in the Kitchen Garden

The garden team are reviving historic horticultural practice, including the advancing and retarding of crops. But there are a few significant changes from William Cresswell's time. In particular, it was not feasible to re-fit a full heating system to the glasshouses, so the full regime of plant forcing of the Victorian period cannot be matched. The full-time gardeners now number only four, instead of eight, though the garden attracts many willing volunteers to help out. Wages have risen a little from Cresswell's 2s 8d (13p) per day. And one of Cresswell's favourite activities, the fumigation of glasshouse plants with his home-produced tobacco, has been replaced by more health-conscious methods!

Turning back time – the restored Kitchen Garden at Audley End now looks like it would have done in the 19th century

Nick Hill, English Heritage
Project Manager 1998–2001 of the Audley End Kitchen Garden Restoration Project

Plant list

The following list is an interpretation of William Cresswell's plant records from his diaries. As we don't have access to William's gardening books and journals, in some cases we will never know exactly what plant he was referring to, so a 'best guess' has been used in those situations. William's spelling of plant names sometimes varied from one page to another and as with other often-used terms, he sometimes rather cryptically abbreviated common plant names.

The majority of plants he used and grew are exactly the same as today, however the botanical names have often changed completely. New plants were being introduced into Britain, or identified in the wild, and several botanists had, independently of each other, named the same plant differently. Until all these differently named, yet identical, plants had been compared against each other, their incorrect names remained in use – often for a number of years until the names were updated in literature. The old name is then referred to as a 'synonym'. Today, changes of names are more likely to be connected to the work of botanists and taxonomists using molecular and genetic techniques to reclassify plants that had been previously grouped together incorrectly using only their physical attributes as a guide.

Above: Cabbage, Autumn green;
below: Sea kale, Crambe maritima;
page 162: A fine floral display in what
was known as the Greenhouse in
Cresswell's time

DIARY ENTRY	COMMON NAME	BOTANICAL NAME
VEGETABLES		
Asparagus	Common asparagus	*Asparagus officinalis*
Bean (Beck's Dwarf Green Gem)		*Vicia faba*
Beet	Common beet	*Beta vulgaris*
Broccoli	Broccoli	*Brassica oleracea*
Brussel sprouts (Roseberry)	Brussel sprouts	*Brassica oleracea*
Cabbage (Savoy; Stewart's Early; Veitch's Early Autumn)	Cabbage	*Brassica oleracea*
Capisum	Common capsicum	*Capsicum annuum*
Carrot (Horn)	Carrot	*Daucus carota*
Cauliflower (Asiatic; Veitch's Autumn Giant)	Cauliflower	*Brassica oleracea*
Celery (Sandringham; Hooley's Conqueror)	Celery	*Apium graveolens*
Colewort	Colewort	*Brassica oleracea*
Cucumber (Ridge; Tree)	Cucumber	*Cucumis sativus*
Endive	Endive	*Cichorium endivia*
French bean (Newington Wonder)	French bean	*Phaseolus vulgaris*
Kail	Kale	*Brassica napus*
Kidney bean	Kidney bean	*Phaseolus vulgaris*
Leek	Leek	*Allium porrum*
Lettuce (Brown Cos; Hammersmith; Hardy Cos; Tom Thumb; Winter Cos)	Lettuce	*Lactuca sativa*
Mangel wurzel	Common beet	*Beta vulgaris*
Marrow	Marrow	*Cucurbita pepo*
Mushroom	Mushroom	
Mustard & Cress	Mustard & cress	*Brassica juncea & Lepidium sativum*
Onion (Giant Tripoli; White Spanish)	Onion	*Allium cepa*

DIARY ENTRY	COMMON NAME	BOTANICAL NAME
Pea (Laxtons Supreme; Carters Surprise; Carters Leviathan; Sancesters No. 1)	Pea	*Pisum sativum*
Potato (Dalmahoy; Early Rose; River's Royal Ash Leaf; Suttons Red-skinned Flourball)	Potato	*Solanum tuberosum*
Radish	Radish	*Raphanus sativus*
Red beet	Common beet	*Beta vulgaris*
Runner bean	Runner bean	*Phaseolus coccineus*
Shallot	Shallot	*Allium cepa*
Spinach	Spinach	*Spinacia oleracea*
Tomato (The Trophy)	Tomato	*Lycopersicon esculentum*
Turnip (Early Store)	Turnip	*Brassica rapa*

FRUIT

Apple (Red Quarrenden)	Apple	*Malus domestica*
Apricot	Apricot	*Prunus armeniaca*
Cherry (Morello)	Morello cherry	*Prunus cerasus* 'Morello'
Currant	Blackcurrant	*Ribes nigrum*
	Redcurrant	*Ribes rubrum*
Fig	Fig	*Ficus carica*
Gooseberry	Gooseberry	*Ribes uva-crispa*
Grape (Muscat; Gros Colman; Lady Downes)	Grape vine	*Vitis vinifera* 'Muscat'; *Vitis vinifera* 'Lady Downe's Seedling'; *Vitis vinifera* 'Gros Colman'
Melon	Melon	*Cucumis melo*
Nectarine	Nectarine	*Prunus persica* var. *nectarina*
Peach	Peach	*Prunus persica*
Pear	Pear	*Pyrus communis*

Espalier-trained apples in the Kitchen Garden at Audley End

DIARY ENTRY	COMMON NAME	BOTANICAL NAME
Plum	Plum	*Prunus domestica*
Raspberry	Raspberry	*Rubus idaeus*
Rhubarb	Garden rhubarb	*Rheum x hybridum*
Strawberry (Black Prince; President; Reen's Seedling)	Strawberry	*Fragaria x ananassa*

PLANTS

Abutilon pictum 'Thompsonii'	Abutilon 'Thompsonii'	*Abutilon pictum* 'Thompsonii'
Acacia coceinea	Scarlet tasselflower	*Emilia coccinea*
Acacia lophantha	Cape wattle	*Paraserianthes lophantha*
Achimenes	Hot water plant	*Achimenes*
Adiantum	Maidenhair fern	*Adiantum*
Adiantum farleyense	Maidenhair fern 'Farleyense'	*Adiantum tenerum* 'Farleyense'
Ageratum	Ageratum	*Ageratum*
Ageratum (Tom Thumb)		Could be an old cultivar, or a reference to the smallest pot size 'Tom Thumb', 'thimble' or 'thumb'
Ageratum, A lophantha		*Paraserianthes lophantha*
Allysum (variegated)	Alyssum	*Alyssum*
Alocasia metallica	Metallic taro	*Alocasia plumbea*
Alocasis macroriza variegate	Giant taro	*Alocasia macrorrhiza* 'Variegata'
Alocasia/Alosia		*Alocasia/Aloysia*
Alosia citriodona	Lemon verbena	*Aloysia triphylla*
Alternanthera		*Alternanthera*
Amaranthus salicifolius & globe		*Amaranthus salicifolius* and *Gomphrena globosa*
Amarillis		*Amaryllis*

A basket of freshly picked plums

DIARY ENTRY	COMMON NAME	BOTANICAL NAME
Anthurium		*Anthurium*
Antirrinhum		*Antirrhinum*
Aralia Veithchii		*Schefflera veitchii*
Araucaria	Monkey Puzzle	*Araucaria araucana*
Aster		*Aster*
Atraucalia excelsa	Norfolk Island pine	*Araucaria heterophylla*
Auricula	Auricula	*Primula auricula*
Azalea		*Azalea*
Balsam		*Impatiens balsamina*
Begonia		*Begonia*
Borage		*Borage*
Bougainvillia		*Bougainvillea*
Bougainvillea glabra	Paper flower	*Bougainvillea glabra*
Bouvardia		*Bouvardia*
Box	Common box	*Buxus sempervirens*
Cacia coceinea	Scarlet tasselflower	*Emilia coccinea*
Cadyline banksii		*Cordyline banksii*
Caladium		*Caladium*
Calamus elegans		*Calamus viridispinus* var. *viridispinus*
Calceolaria		*Calceolaria*
Camellia		*Camellia*
Candidissima Tansonia van Volsomi		*Tamonea*? If so, could relate to another synonym of *Miconia calvescens*
Canna		*Canna*
Celosia japonica	Common Cock's Comb	*Celosia argentea*
Centaurea		*Centaurea*
Centaurea gymnocarpa		*Centaurea cineraria*
Centaurea clementii		*Centaurea clementei*

Low hedges of box make an effective and attractive edge to borders

DIARY ENTRY	COMMON NAME	BOTANICAL NAME
Centaurea ragusina Centaurea ragusina compacta		*Centaurea ragusina*
Chloris radiata		*Agrostis radiata*
Chrysanthemum		*Chrysanthemum*
Cineraria		*Senecio*
Cineraria maritima	Silver ragwort	*Senecio cineraria*
Cleredendron balfourii	Bleeding glory bower	*Clerodendrum thomsoniae*
Clerodendron fallax splendens		*Clerodendrum speciosissimum*
Clianthus		*Clianthus*
Coecinea		A specific epithet – *coccinea*
Coleus	Coleus	*Solenostemon scutellarioides*
Colosia japonica	Common cock's comb	*Celosia argentea*
Coproenia baureana	Looking glass plant	*Coprosma repens*
Coranilla		*Coranilla*
Croton pictum	Croton	*Codiaeum variegatum* var. *pictum*
Cyanophyllum magnificum	Velvet tree	*Miconia calvescens*
Cyclamen		*Cyclamen*
Cyclamen corsicum		*Colchicum corsicum*
C. persicum	Persian cyclamen	*Cyclamen persicum*
D. guilfoilii	Cabbage palm	*Cordyline australis*
Dahlia		*Dahlia*
Dampierii	Desert pea	*Swainsona formosa*
Delphinium formosum		*Delphinium formosum*
Deutzia gracilis	Japanese snow flower	*Deutzia gracilis*
Diffenbachia		*Dieffenbachia*
Dracaena cooperi	Cabbage tree	*Cordyline fruticosa*
Dracaenia		*Dracaena*

The elegant canna lilly – a fashionable Victorian plant

DIARY ENTRY	COMMON NAME	BOTANICAL NAME
Dracaena (Amabilis)		*Dracaena* x *amabilis*
Echevera metallica	Metallic echeveria	*Echeveria gibbiflora* var. *metallica*
Echeveria retusa sinensis		*Echeveria retusa*
Epacris		*Epacris*
Epyphyllum		*Epiphyllum*
Erica hymalis	French heather	*Erica* x *hiemalis*
Eschyanthus		*Aeschynanthus*
Eucharis amazonica	Amazon lily	*Eucharis amazonica*
Euphorbia		*Euphorbia*
Euphorbia jacquiniflora	Scarlet plume	*Euphorbia fulgens*
Fern (Maiden hair)	Common maidenhair fern	*Adiantum aethiopicum*
Fuchsia		*Fuchsia*
Fuchsia Sunray		*Fuchsia* 'Sunray'
G. amarathus	Globe amaranth	*Gomphrena globosa*
G. Jean Sisley		*Rosa* 'Jean Sisley' G. could refer to 'Guillot', the French nursery which sold this rose
Genista		*Genista*
Genytilles tulipera		*Genetyllis tulipifera*
Geonoma gracilis	Chachi	*Geonoma cuneata* var.
Geranium (Bayard; Bijou; Bronze; Crystal Palace Gem; Lord Palmerston; Master Christine; Scented; Vesuvius; Victor Lemoine; Vyde Lyon; zonal)		*Pelargonium* cultivars
Gesneria		*Gesneria*
Gesneria exoniensis		*Gesneria* x *exoniensis*
Globe amaranthus	Globe amaranth	*Gomphrena globosa*
Gloxinia		*Gloxinia*
Golden Pyrethum		*Tanacetum parthenium* 'Golden Moss' or similar

Dahlias are as popular today as they were in the 1870s

DIARY ENTRY	COMMON NAME	BOTANICAL NAME
Golden Starwort		*Aster* sp.
Heath		*Erica* sp.
Heather		*Erica* sp.
Heliotrope		*Heliotropium*
Hollyhock	Hollyhock	*Alcea rosea*
Honesty	Honesty	*Lunaria annua*
Hyacinth (Early Roman)		*Hyacinthus orientalis*
Hydrangea		*Hydrangea*
Iresine		*Iresine*
Iresine lindeni	Blood leaf	*Iresine lindenii*
Isolepis gracilis		*Ficinia nodosa*
Lachenalia tricolor	Opal flower	*Lachenalia aloides*
Lemaria gibba	Miniature tree fern	*Blechnum gibbum*
Lily of the Valley	Lily of the valley	*Convallaria majalis*
Lobelia speciosa pumila		*Lobelia* x *speciosa*
Locasia lowii		*Alocasia longiloba*
Lomaria gibba	Miniature tree fern	*Blechnum gibbum*
Lycopodium Lycopodium denticulatum	Kraus's clubmoss	*Selaginella kraussiana*
Lycopodium Caesia	Peacock moss	*Selaginella uncinata*
Maranta veitchii	Peacock Plant	*Calathea veitchiana*
Mignonette	Mignonette	*Reseda odorata*
Mignonette (Dwarf; Hybrid Tea)		There is a polyantha rose 'Mignonette' however it was bred later in 1881
Monophylla (Kennedy's)	Vine lilac	*Hardenbergia violacea* (syn. *Kennedia monophylla*)
Myosotis		
Myosotis dissitiflora		*Myosotis dissitiflora*
Myrtle	Common myrtle	*Myrtus communis*
Narcissus		*Narcissus*

Hollyhock flowers have a wide variety of different colours, this is Alcea rosea

DIARY ENTRY	COMMON NAME	BOTANICAL NAME
Oleander		*Oleander*
P. Golden Feather		*Celosia argentea* var. *cristata* Plumosa Group 'Golden Feather'
Pansy	Pansy	*Viola tricolor*
Pariensis		*Geonoma paraensis*
Pelargonium (Snowdrop/Gauntlet)	See *Geranium*	
Perilla		*Perilla*
Phenocoma statico profusa	Pink everlasting	*Phaenocoma prolifera*
Phlox		*Phlox*
Pilea muscosa	Artillery plant	*Pilea microphylla*
Pink		*Dianthus*
Poinsettia Poinsettia pulcherima	Poinsettia	*Euphorbia pulcherrima*
Poinsettia pulcherisima		
Poleanthus		*Polyanthus*
Polemonium		*Polemonium*
Primrose	Primrose	*Primula vulgaris*
Primula		*Primula*
Primula (Chinese)	Chinese primrose	*Primula sinensis*
Primula sinensis		
Privet	Garden privet	*Ligustrum vulgare*
Pteris tremula	Australian brake	*Pteris tremula*
Richardia ethiopica	Arum lily	*Zantedeschia aethiopica*
Rose (Marechal Niel; Gloiry de Dijon)		*Rosa* 'Maréchal Niel' *Rosa* 'Gloire de Dijon'
Salera patens	Gentian sage	*Salvia patens*
Salvia		*Salvia*
Salvia splendens	Scarlet sage	*Salvia splendens*
Saxifraga cassifolia	Elephant ears	*Bergenia crassifolia*
Scherzerianum	Flamingo Flower	*Anthurium*

Purple sage, Salvia officinalis *'Purpurascens'*

Above: Victorian-style exotic planting
Opposite: *The Vinery range – full of plants as it would have been in William Cresswell's time*

DIARY ENTRY	COMMON NAME	BOTANICAL NAME
Selaginella caesia	Peacock Moss	*Selaginella uncinata*
Selaginella denticulata	Kraus's clubmoss	*Selaginella kraussiana*
Solanum hybridum		*Solanum hybridum*
Sparrmannia africana	African Hemp	*Sparrmannia africana*
Sphaerogyne Sphaerogene latifolia		*Tococa platyphylla*
Stellaria graminea aurea	Lesser stitchwort	*Stellaria graminea* 'Aurea'
Stephanotis		*Stephanotis*
Stephanotis floribunda	Stephanotis	*Stephanotis floribunda*
Stock (Brompton)	Brompton stock	*Matthiola incana*
Stoloniferum		*Selaginella plumosa*
Sunchezia nobilis	Shrubby whitevein	*Sanchezia speciosa*
Sweet William	Sweet William	*Dianthus barbatus*
Tagetes signata pumila	Border of gold	*Tagetes tenuifolia* 'Pumila'
Torenia asiatica		*Torenia asiatica*
Tradescantia		*Tradescantia*
Tree carnation		Probably refers to a 'perpetual flowering carnation'
Tulip		*Tulipa*
Verbena (Boule de Neige; Lemon-scented)		*Aloysia triphylla*
Viola (Mauve Queen; Lutea)	Mountain pansy	*Viola lutea*
Violet		*Viola*
Wall flower	Common wallflower	*Erysimum cheiri*
Zinnia (single & double)		*Zinnia*

ACKNOWLEDGEMENTS

This book owes a great deal to Patricia Beatrice Rabôt, the great granddaughter of William Cresswell, whose help, constant support and encouragement has been very much appreciated.

Many other people have helped and their assistance is gratefully acknowledged – in particular: Rowan Blaik for horticultural research and editing; John W Brown who supplied a wealth of information and illustrations from his archives; Judith Dobie, English Heritage, for the beautiful line drawings illustrating the Diary section; Nick Hill, English Heritage, for commenting on the text; Gareth Hughes, English Heritage, for his support and guidance; Chris Hull for the photographs specially taken for this book; Christine Jennings for sharing her knowledge of the history of Grantchester with us, and allowing us to use her book *Widnall: A Capital Contriver – The story of a Victorian household in the village of Grantchester*; and Teresa Widd who checked the proofs and made valuable comments on the text.

We would also like to thank for their help and advice: Ann Ash; Katie Bryan; Adèle Campbell; Mike Thurlow, Garden Organic; Phillippa Mapes; Philip Norman, Museum of Garden History, London; Jill Palmer, Saffron Walden Library; Fiona Parish, Cambridge Central Library; Quincy Rabôt; René Rodgers, Rebecca Smith and Andrew Widd.

Lady Braybrooke's letter quoted on pp 20–1 and 128 is in the collection of the Essex Record Office (ERO, Acc 8422, Box 11/20, item 19).

PICTURE CREDITS

May | 1884

W | 27 | Wind S.E. bright & very warm
Verbenas planted out in beds
Potted Gesneria's singly in large 60s
started in stove with bottom heat
to be shifted on as required. Put
in cuttings of Pelargoniums (early)
Varieties Snowdrop & Gauntlet

T | 28 | Wind S. very warm, plenty of air
not much sun, clouds indicative
of storms, Geraniums (Vesuvius
& Bayard) put out, Shifted young
plts of Echevera retusa sinensis
into 32s for winter blooming, Repotted
large Camellia's in Green-house
Ceased syringing earliest peaches
which are now nearly ripe, Cherry
tree in Orchard house pulled up,
on walls

Capsicums potted
off & put in cucumber
frame till rooted